The Encroaching Desert

The Encroaching Desert

The Consequences of Human Failure

A Report for the Independent Commission on International Humanitarian Issues

Zed Books Ltd
London and New Jersey

This report does not necessarily reflect the views, individually or collectively, of the members of the Independent Commission on International Humanitarian Issues (ICIHI). It is based on research carried out for ICIHI and was prepared under the supervision of its Secretariat with the guidance of the ICIHI Working Group on Disasters.

The Encroaching Desert was first published by Zed Books Ltd.,
57 Caledonian Road, London N1 9BU and
171 First Avenue, Atlantic Highlands, New Jersey 07716, in 1986.

© Secretariat of the Independent Commission on International Humanitarian Issues, 1986

Cover design by Henry Iles
Cover photography: Riverbed, Timia Sahara, Niger
Mark Edwards, Earthscan
Typeset by EMS Photosetters, Rochford, Essex
Printed and bound in Great Britain by
Cox and Wyman Ltd., Reading

British Library Cataloguing in Publication Data

The Encroaching desert: the consequences of human failure:
a report for the Independent Commission on International
Humanitarian Issues.
1. Desertification
I. Independent Commission on International Humanitarian Issues   II. La Désertification *English*
333.73   GB611

ISBN 0-86232-633-8
ISBN 0-86232-634-6 Pbk

Contents

The Independent Commission on International Humanitarian Issues

Co-Chairmen:

Sadruddin Aga Khan (Iran)   Hassan bin Talal (Jordan)

Members:

Susanna Agnelli	(Italy)
Talal Bin Abdul Aziz Al Saud	(Saudi Arabia)
Paulo Evaristo Arns, Vice-Chairman	(Brazil)
Mohammed Bedjaoui	(Algeria)
Henrik Beer, Treasurer	(Sweden)
Luis Echeverria Alvarez	(Mexico)
Pierre Graber	(Switzerland)
Ivan Head	(Canada)
M. Hidayatullah	(India)
Aziza Hussein	(Egypt)
Manfred Lachs	(Poland)
Robert McNamara	(USA)
Lazar Mojsov	(Yugoslavia)
Mohamed Mzali, Vice-Chairman	(Tunisia)
Sadako Ogata, Vice-Chairman	(Japan)
David Owen	(United Kingdom)
Willibald P. Pahr, Vice-Chairman	(Austria)
Shridath S. Ramphal	(Guyana)
Ru Xin	(China)
Salim A. Salim	(Tanzania)
Léopold Sédar Senghor	(Senegal)
Soedjatmoko	(Indonesia)
Desmond Tutu	(South Africa)
Simone Veil	(France)
Gough Whitlam	(Australia)

Secretary-General, ex-officio member:
Zia Rizvi (Pakistan)

Other ICIHI Reports

FAMINE: A Man-Made Disaster? (Pan Books, London/ Sydney, 1985). Other language editions: Arabic, French, Italian, Japanese, Portuguese, Serbo-Croatian and Spanish.

THE VANISHING FOREST (Zed Books, London, 1986). Other language editions: Arabic, French and Serbo-Croatian.

STREET CHILDREN: A Growing Urban Tragedy (Weidenfeld & Nicolson, London, 1986). Other language editions: Arabic, French, Japanese, and Spanish.

Other reports to be published in 1986 include:
    Humanitarian Norms and Armed Conflicts
    Refugees
    Disappeared Persons
    Statelessness
    Autochthonous People

ICIHI Working Group on Disasters

The following members of the Independent Commission helped in the preparation of this report in their individual capacities:

Sadruddin Aga Khan	(Iran)
Mohammed Bedjaoui	(Algeria)
Henrik Beer	(Sweden)
Manfred Lachs	(Poland)
Sadako Ogata	(Japan)
David Owen	(United Kingdom)

Drafting Committee

L. Timberlake (Editor)
assisted by R. Clarke

in consultation with:

P. Bifani	P. Spitz
Z. Rizvi	B. Walker

Foreword

Desertification is a particularly devastating form of environmental deterioration afflicting arid and semi-arid areas. Its causes have been analysed and various solutions have been advanced. This Report establishes that the struggle against desertification has failed to produce satisfactory results and attempts to identify the causes of this failure at both the national and international levels. It is not proposed here to summarize the arguments put forth, but to offer additional clarification concerning the concept, or rather the concepts, of time in nature and society.

A keen observation of nature reveals that each ecosystem develops according to its own particular rhythm determined by the dynamics of the living organisms existing within it as well as by climatic, soil, water and atmospheric changes. The development of human societies naturally has an impact on each of these factors, whether direct or indirect, immediate or long-term.

The complexity of these interactions requires an interdisciplinary analysis based on continuous and regular observation. A constant monitoring of the development of major physiochemical and biological environmental factors, and their relationships with social, cultural and economic factors, can promote a better understanding of the development of nature and society in relation to each other, and a more accurate forecasting of the consequences of human intervention. As a result, wiser choices could be

11

made from among the various possible economic and social policies for rural areas. This continuous monitoring would also permit the detection of abnormal developments and thereby lay the groundwork for an effective warning system.

Farmers and herdsmen who depend upon these ecosystems for a living have their own particular view of these changes. Their period of observation is that of their adolescence and adulthood. Vague childhood memories are supplemented by the stories their parents tell. From generation to generation, links are thus established in a chain of observations concerning the evolution of herds and land, water and desert, rainfall and drought. It is because of uncertainty that farmers and herdsmen are forced to make decisions whose consequences become increasingly serious as their economic resources decrease and their natural environment gets more fragile. The very existence of the family is then at stake. The critical nature of this struggle for human survival can never be sufficiently emphasized.

Collective memory centres upon tragic events such as famines, droughts and locust devastations. It also has a tendency to reconstruct a very distant golden age mourned by the elders. Time references such as these, despite their subjective nature, allowed people to organize empirical knowledge, develop strategies to tackle recurring disasters and adapt technical, social and legal regulations to ecosystem changes. However, this was only possible at a time when changes were sufficiently slow to enable adjustments between nature and society gradually to take their own course.

The Bedouins have inherited a long tradition of observing desert conditions, climate and populations. This has enabled them to become skilful users of scarce resources in an environment where few experts, however laden with university degrees, could survive.

In the course of the last few decades, the ecosystems of arid and semi-arid countries have become subjected to swift changes. Desertification stands as a witness to the rapidly growing imbalances. The role of the State has thus become essential in re-establishing the balances between the ecosystems and the populations which depend upon them for a living. Farmers and nomads faced with the requirements of daily survival may have no choice but to further destroy their vital environment.

Reconstruction is more time-consuming than destruction. It behoves the State to safeguard the nation's long-term interests by preserving natural resources for future generations and by reconstituting soil fertility before it is too late. At the same time, the State must provide short-term assistance for those whose livelihoods are threatened by desertification.

A wealth of modern practical and scientific knowledge is available for that purpose. However, the extraordinary development of that knowledge during this century has contributed to the concealment and neglect of the potential value of the empirical environmental knowledge stored by those who are in touch with daily reality.

There is an urgent need to submit this precious knowledge and ensuing practices to modern scientific analysis and to organize a continuous dialogue between scientists, administrators, farmers and herdsmen.

Such a dialogue must be accompanied by a deep commitment on the part of responsible authorities at all levels. They must devote all their energy to ensuring a more stable food supply for the least privileged groups of society while preserving the nation's long-term biological and economic natural resources. Only through such efforts can solutions be found in the struggle against desertification; efforts which respect the vital interests of today's farmers and herdsmen as well as those of their descendants.

Hassan bin TALAL
Crown Prince of Jordan
Co-Chairman of ICIHI

Editorial Note

When the Independent Commission on International Humanitarian Issues decided to establish a Working Group on Disasters in 1984, famine was spreading across Africa. It was natural for the Commission to address the humanitarian aspects of this tragic situation. The discussions which followed led to the preparation of three reports:

Famine: A Man-Made Disaster?, Pan Books, London/ Sydney, 1985; *The Vanishing Forest: The Human Consequences of Deforestation*, Zed Books, London, 1986; and the present report on desertification.

We wish to thank L. Timberlake who, with the help of R. Clarke, prepared the draft. The comments made by the members of the Commission, in particular those participating in its Working Group on Disasters, are reflected in the Report. It was reviewed by members of the Secretariat of the Commission. Paolo Bifani and Pierre Spitz contributed significantly to its finalization: M. El Kouhene, B. Balmer and D. Topali, of the Secretariat, helped in the technical preparation of the Report. R. Molteno and Zed Books provided valuable assistance in the publication of the Report.

Any income from sales of this book will be devoted entirely to research on humanitarian issues.

H. Beer
Convenor, Working Group
on Disasters

Z. Rizvi
Secretary-General

Geneva, April 1986

Introduction

The accelerated process of desertification has reached a dimension that is largely surpassing the traditional approach to the problem. Desertification has become a natural and social disaster with many humanitarian aspects that require adequate attention and prompt action. Therefore any meaningful discussion has to go beyond the main techno-cratic aspects which predominate in past approaches. A deteriorating natural environment and the dire poverty of the population in the areas at risk also reflect the failure of the international community to prevent and control desertification. Recent estimates show that 230 million people are directly threatened by desertification. Altogether, 3.5 billion hectares of the world's rainfed cropland and irrigated land are affected and every year a further 21 million hectares are reduced to a state of near or complete uselessness.

Yet, despite the magnitude of the threat, people, their leaders and their organizations have shown little ability or willingness to tackle the problem.

This Report analyses the factors behind their failure. Some involve political shortsightedness and ineptitude, others are the inevitable result of an unfortunate concurrence of international and natural events. These factors include:

(a) *Failure to see desertification in context* and as part of the socio-economic development of arid and semi-arid regions, i.e. failure to grasp the global character of desertification.

(b) *Failure of the developing countries* affected to explicitly incorporate the problem in their programmes of rural development, and, in general, in the context of development planning.

(c) *A wrong approach to the problem:* Actions have been geared more to the consequences than to the causes, and lately only to alleviate shortages or hardship caused by desertification. Very little action, if any, has been taken to create, and even less to implement, alternative strategies. In other words, the causes of desertification have not been dealt with. No solutions have been provided to avoid deforestation, reduce overgrazing or excessive use of the land, develop irrigation schemes suitable for arid soil, or develop and adopt the right kind of technology for the conditions of arid and semi-arid ecosystems and for local cultural, social and economic patterns.

(d) *Near or total absence of activities oriented to people or involving their participation:* This deficiency is reflected in the total lack of projects for a better understanding of socio-economic aspects of desertification; the lack of progress in the monitoring of human conditions in desertified lands and of populations at risk; the total absence of efforts to elaborate social indicators of desertification; absolute absence of projects oriented to the creation of economic alternatives in arid lands that can contribute to alleviating the pressure in desertification–prone areas; lack of projects involving community participation and absence of actions for the creation of institutions and conditions for people participation.

(e) *Lack of action-oriented corrective projects:* The large number of projects implemented by the international community embrace complementary, supportive, or pre-paratory activities (monitoring, training, preparation of activities, reports, etc). Very few projects have been designed for concrete corrective action and fewer still have been implemented.

(f) *Unfavourable climatic conditions* – mainly the recurrent drought – that have affected several desertification–prone areas of the world and, in particular, the Sudano–Sahelian countries.

(g) *The simultaneous arrival of a number of inter-related international setbacks*, including a major recession, decreasing commodity prices and increasingly poor terms of trade for developing countries, the debt repayment crisis, and cutbacks in support for, and accordingly aid from, multilateral organizations.

(h) *Failure by the international community* to provide enough financial and technical assistance and the right kind of aid under sufficiently flexible and favourable terms.

(i) *Poor co-ordination of efforts* by the relevant co-ordinating and implementing United Nations bodies and failure by these bodies to raise appropriate funds.

(j) *Counter-productive inter-agency rivalry* between many of the regional and international bodies involved in the fight against desertification.

The current renewed drought in the Sahel and the Horn of Africa, and the drought in Southern and East Africa, have served to highlight the failure of efforts against desertification. However, in the nine years since the United Nations Conference on Desertification (UNCOD) formulated its Plan of Action to Combat Desertification, swift and efficient action would unquestionably have saved many thousands of lives and avoided considerable human suffering.

1. The Humanitarian Aspects of Desertification

Man is both the cause and the victim of desertification, a process which is continuing or even accelerating in Africa, Asia and Latin America — in fact, everywhere, except in the temperate croplands of Mediterranean Europe, North America and Australia.

Desertification is a dynamic process not necessarily exclusive of any particular region. Erosion, salinization, waterlogging, etc, can and do occur in different places and on different types of land. The areas prone to desertification are said to include 27 million hectares of irrigated farmland, 173 million hectares of rainfed cropland and a little over 3 billion hectares of rangeland. Desertification is therefore a threat for mankind as a whole in that it reduces the sustainable base of society at large. Right now, however, desertification is already a disaster for those populations directly affected, living in the most deprived areas of the world. They have lost their livelihood, and suffered a sharp deterioration in their nutritional and health status. Whole communities have also been deprived of their economic activities; their social institutions have been disrupted and their most productive members have had to migrate and seek relocation elsewhere.

Because the term desertification sounds like a natural and localized phenomenon, the public and many decision-makers have tended to regard it as an inherently ecological and physical problem affecting desertified regions only, especially in Africa. There is always an image of wind-struck sand dunes, barren and hostile expanses uninhabited but for a few nomadic groups.

Arid lands and *deserts* are expressions frequently used as synonymous to designate certain areas, and drought is seen as an inseparable element. Yet areas affected by desertification are neither unproductive nor empty. Furthermore, arid areas are not doomed to desertification, which is a symptom — probably the most dramatic symptom — of the lack of development of particular parts of the world.

But what are *arid lands*? The expression refers to areas with a very dry climate, including steppes in temperate zones and pampas and savannas in tropical and sub-tropical regions. According to experts, arid lands cover around 35% of the world's land surface. *Deserts* are areas with an extremely arid climate, very irregular precipitation and excessive evaporation. In these areas, organic life is restricted to a very meagre fauna and flora. *Desertification* has been used to describe the spread of desert surface and the reduction of the potential productivity of the affected areas. It implies a widespread deterioration of ecosystems and destruction of their biological productivity, ultimately resulting in the absence of perennial life.

Drought is seen by the lay person as a problem of water shortage due to insufficient rainfall for a certain period of time. The absence or shortage of rain and the temporary character of the problem are the most visible elements. However, the problem is apparently more complex. In theory, water shortage can be the result of weather or climatic change and, in fact, scientists are accepting that drought must be viewed as a recurring and periodic phenomenon, to be examined also from its economic and social perspective and therefore not only in terms of the levels of precipitation in a given place. So a distinction has frequently been made between meteorological drought, which refers to the rains failing to reach a certain level over a particular period of time in a given area, and agricultural drought which refers to the fact that the combined effects of amounts and distribution of rainfall, soil water reserves and evaporation bring about a drastic reduction of agricultural yields and livestock leading to food scarcity and other associated problems.

At the United Nations Conference on Desertification (UNCOD) in 1977, desertification was defined as 'the diminution or destruction of the biological potential of the land, which leads ultimately to desert-like conditions and is an aspect of the widespread deterioration of ecosystems under the combined pressure of adverse and fluctuating climate and excessive exploitation'.

This deterioration process affects different types of land: irrigated rainfed land and rangelands. Irrigated land deterioration is reflected in the spread and increasing accumulation of salt in the soil, a phenomenon known as salinization, increasing saturation of the soil with sodium, a phenomenon called alkalinization, overpumping of aquifers, waterlogging and wasteful loss of water through evaporation. All these phenomena reinforce each other and lead to the reduction of the productive capacity of soil. In drylands the deterioration is manifested basically by the increasing erosion of land, the reduction of the vegetative cover and consequently of organic material, the insufficient fallow period and the slow spread of sand into the fields.

Finally, the degeneration of rangelands is reflected in the thinning of the herbaceous cover, the spread of bush and non-fodder vegetable species, the increasingly ephemeral nature of herbaceous resources and the lengthening of recuperation after the 'normal' drought season.

Desertification is a socio-economic and natural process which reduces the fertility and biological productivity of the soil to the level which characterizes deserts. It is one of the clearest results of the close and increasing inter-relationships between social and natural systems. Though desertification affects mainly arid and semi-arid areas, it is also found elsewhere. It is the result of a long historical process through which natural phenomena and human activities reinforce each other in changing the characteristics of natural environments. Throughout the history of mankind, arid and semi-arid regions have provided a habitat for large communities which have developed institutional mechanisms, life styles and socio-economic patterns according to the constraints and potentialities of surrounding natural systems.

During recent decades, concern has been increasing because desertification has accelerated with dramatic consequences for mankind, and in particular, for the 230 million people directly affected. These are located mainly in developing countries, where the process worsens an already serious socio-economic situation. Governments are confronted with increasing difficulties in their response because of slow development.

There is a serious dilemma: if sufficient resources are not provided immediately to cope with the present dramatic situation, many people may starve to death. But if the structural causes of the problem are not dealt with today, more resources will be needed tomorrow to alleviate the plight of an even greater mass of deprived people and not just to cope with increasing environmental deterioration. What makes things worse is the magnitude of the humanitarian issues at stake. There is a need for urgent action, but the affected countries simply do not have the resources for that. Nor has the international community been able to find them or channel an appropriate amount to those most in need. The difficult questions are: how to deal with the present without jeopardizing the future, how to harmonize the palliative action of today with the preventive and corrective strategies aiming at the root causes and how to devise mutually supportive short and long-term policies.

There are therefore humanitarian aspects both in the short and in the long term. The most obvious humanitarian aspects of desertification are related to lack of resources, regressive income distribution, increasing poverty, hunger and malnutrition, poor health, extinction of communities, disruption of traditional life-styles and economic patterns, migration, marginalization.

The short-term humanitarian aspects are very visible and motivate international action mainly in the form of aid, to alleviate the affected population. However, in the long term, desertification is affecting the very process of development, because it reduces the natural system's carrying capacity. At the same time, environmental deterioration is a main cause of social and economic insecurity, resulting in greater vulnerability to both natural and man-made hazards. Social and economic security can be achieved only by long-term integral and sustainable development.

It has been said that desertification is a long-term physical and pervasive phenomenon caused by human action over the natural environment and in particular in arid and semi-arid lands. According to some experts, even if past history shows that the role of man in desertification is minor compared to that of nature, there is no doubt that the acceleration of the trend over the past century, and especially over the past fifty years, is associated with the land-use practices and changes which followed the integration of the societies of arid and semi-arid regions in the international system.

The opinion that desertification is basically a natural phenomenon is sustained among others by a recent report prepared by Dr F. El-Baz and Dr T.A. Maxwell for NASA. But even this approach should be examined carefully. In fact, in their study of the Dar el Arba Desert, it is said that: 'it should be abundantly clear that the role of man in desertification is minor compared to that of natural change. In fact, except for the sensitive fringe areas and the cases where ground water is being over-exploited, his role is insignificant. But these are the only inhabited areas of deserts, so, from a provincial point of view, the result of man's activities can be disastrous.' The second part of this quotation is important to the extent that it supports the approach adopted in the present Report which views natural phenomena in relation to their human dimension.

The changes in production patterns and related land-use practices of dryland societies following their increasing integration into the international economic system are underlying causes of the acceleration of desertification. The acceleration is also triggered or exacerbated by changes in the dynamics of the natural environment and societies, and specifically by natural recurrent phenomena like drought and by changes in population dynamics.

Since all the causal factors are mutually inter-dependent, they reinforce one another and have a feedback effect which accelerates the whole process.

23

Traditional societies in arid and semi-arid lands develop appropriate economic systems for their fragile and hostile natural environments. Both agricultural and livestock systems evolved practices like crop rotation, pastoral movement and agricultural–livestock combination which ensured a sustainable and renewable use of the environment as well as the recovery of the land's biological productivity.

Given the characteristics of the natural environment and the low level of technological development — and therefore of managerial skills — among local communities, the extremely precarious balance between society and nature is greatly affected by the increasing integration of populations in an international economic system which has failed to provide feasible development alternatives, thus bringing about a socio-economic and environmental crisis instead of development. Traditional agricultural practices gave way to overcultivation, livestock practices to overgrazing, the rational use of natural resources to woodland clearance, and so on.

In short, the socio-economic causes of desertification are related to such inadequate land-use practices as over-cultivation, overgrazing, woodland clearance and mis-management of water resources.

Because of their increasing foreign currency needs, developing countries devote more land to cash crops, shorten fallow times and expand irrigation schemes. More land for cash crops has meant encroaching on marginal land and expelling their traditional users – grazing animals. Such areas were traditionally used only by pastoralists because of their lower productivity. The extension of cash crops has led to crop homogenization or monoculture, of which the best example in arid and semi-arid areas is groundnut monoculture which has had a negative impact on soil productivity. It is reported that in Senegal productivity has fallen from 1 tonne per acre in 1940 to 0.4 tonne per acre in 1980. Moreover, because of unfavourable groundnut prices on international markets, producers striving to maintain their level of income have had to cultivate larger areas, use more marginal lands, thus reducing the area used for food crops and fallow time and increasing soil deterioration.

The expulsion of pastoralists from previous marginal grazing areas changed grazing and nomadic patterns. Basically, more animals graze more frequently on less extensive pastures. Why more animals? First, because pastoralists regard livestock as a resource base and as a safeguard for bad years, and because the demand for meat in many areas adjacent to arid and semi-arid lands has increased. This has also led to the development of ranching for meat production. Ranching schemes have of course followed the Western model.

These ranching schemes failed to take into account the specific conditions of tropical drylands, their relatively lower productivity, and the time needed for the regeneration of pastures. Moreover, they were meat-oriented whereas the traditional economy had always been milk-oriented. Ranching has been introduced in most cases as an enclave with no relation to the local pastoralists who were in fact expelled. Nor was it suited to the environment or the existing socio-economic system.

The deforestation of arid lands is an additional cause of desertification. According to the FAO, deforestation of arid lands affects 4 million hectares per year, of which 2.7 million are in Africa, and is due partly to the reduction of pastures and partly to the increasing demand for fuelwood which has been accelerated by urban expansion. Woodland clearance for charcoal production is indeed one of the main causes of dryland deforestation. Wood, charcoal and agricultural waste meet almost 100% of household energy needs in the Sahel; indeed 82% of the total energy used by the eight Sahel countries comes from wood. According to the FAO, the present shortage of fuelwood in arid regions is equivalent to the production of 25.8 million hectares of intensive cultivation of fast-growing fuelwood plantations, and if present trends are not reversed, this shortage will more than double by the year 2000. The shortage affects mainly the Sahel, Sudan, Ethiopia, Kenya, Somalia, India, Pakistan and North-East Brazil. Deforestation in turn contributes to soil deterioration and water scarcity. The denuded arid areas are directly exposed to solar radiation, to the winds and rains, and therefore to increased erosion. Deforestation of

25

watersheds reduces the water retention capacity of the soil which, together with erosion, increases silt deposits and reduces the effectiveness of irrigation schemes and water reservoirs. Things get worse when irrigation schemes do not match dryland conditions. Poor management and water-logging also accelerate soil degradation.

The combined effects of deforestation, water–logging, erosion, etc, finally lead to a fall in the water table and to salinization problems. The misuse of wells — frequent where nomads are resettled — also compounds difficulties.

Where these additional factors are not present, destructive practices are frequently concealed in the short and medium term and only become apparent over a longer period of time. But a natural disaster or social change quickly brings them to light. Drought and demographic change are the usual triggers.

Eroded, over-exploited, over-grazed and deforested arid lands are more vulnerable to drought. Long and recurrent rain failures cause additional soil erosion, thus accelerating the ongoing process of desertification.

During a drought, the wind erodes the denuded and deteriorated soil. When the rains finally do come, the water runs off quickly from a soil that has lost its retention capacity, taking with it organic material and topsoil, and causing floods, with considerable material damage and loss of life.

A report commissioned by the Ethiopian government blamed that country's 1972–74 famine not on 'a drought of unprecedented severity' but on 'a combination of long continued bad land use and steadily increased human and stock populations over decades, rendering a greater number of people and their animals vulnerable when drought struck'.[1] The same is true of Ethiopia's latest drought, all the more so as areas affected by severe desertification are slow to recover, especially if the time span between two periods of drought is short.

The relation between drought and desertification is illustrated by the two following examples.[2]

The Masol Plains of Northwestern Kenya have been largely unoccupied since 1974 when Pokot pastoralists were forced to abandon the area because of raids by neighbouring groups. The plains are a 'zone of insecurity' and act as a buffer between hostile peoples. Droughts have struck the area since 1973, but the lack of rainfall has had no demonstrable effect on the land and no desertification has occurred. In fact, a study of the area concluded that 1973–1978 was a period of generally decreasing rainfall, but acacia bush doubled from 24% to almost 50% of ground cover because herders no longer used the area. The study showed that the vegetation biomass of an area can actually increase during a period of drought.

For the same period, 1973–1978, the situation in Turkana only 150 km north of the Masol Plains was very different. The drought resulted in high levels of stock loss, large displacements of the Turkana population, the impoverishment of tens of thousands of people and a large-scale famine relief effort.

As the biological potential of Turkana land dropped with the drought, animals were forced to eat every available scrap of edible vegetation they could find. Man helped in this process by lopping off leaf-bearing branches and even by chopping down entire trees. The well–known cycle of soil denudation and erosion then set in and countless tonnes of soil were lost. Many of the dispossessed have gone into charcoal production to make a living, further degrading the land.

During the same period of time, under the same climatic conditions of drought, two adjacent areas have therefore experienced completely different types of environmental change. One area increased in vegetation cover, the other suffered increased desertification which resulted in great human suffering. The difference was due to differing land-use practices and population densities in the two areas. Desertification was accelerated by drought in Turkana, but it had no adverse effect on the Masol Plains.

In some cases, defensive measures to mitigate the effects of drought can lead in the long run to the acceleration of desertification. For example, during a drought, deep boreholes attract herders and their herds. Because the water supply at boreholes can be relatively permanent, herds over-

27

graze the area for many kilometers around the well site. Here again it is a case of short-term versus long-term action. Short-term responses, e.g., a quick water supply, may in the long term have adverse effects on the environment. Decision-makers are under pressure to supply water during a drought; but they are often unable to control its use.

The impact of demographic factors on desertification should be examined both from the point of view of density and dynamics.

The population density in arid lands is relatively low compared to that of countries or regions as a whole. It has been shown that there is no direct causal link between growing population density and pressure on drylands.

Although there can be very localized cases of population over-concentration, this should not lead to the hasty conclusion that over-population is a major dryland problem.

It has been reported that, out of 24 countries whose population grew by an average of 3% or more between 1970 and 1978, 15 were suffering from desertification and that every year the combined population of the six main Sahelian countries — Senegal, Mauritania, Mali, Burkina Faso, Niger and Chad — increases by 1.4 million. But these figures should be examined carefully. Indeed the average increase fails to reflect the specific situation of arid and semi-arid areas. In fact, scientific research has shown that fertility is lower in most of the Sahelian countries than in the coastal areas of West Africa, in particular among nomadic people. This has been attributed to a number of reasons. Nomads are aware of the effects of rapid population growth for the rather critical balance between society and the environment. Sexual abstinence is reported in countries like Somalia where marriage takes place later in life, dowries are heavy, and long periods of marital separation common. Another factor frequently mentioned is the high level of disease-induced infertility among nomadic Fulani.

More recently, the declining birth rate in arid lands has also been attributed to temporary female infertility because of malnutrition and absence of spouses. Migration seems to have increased considerably in recent years. The long-lasting drought combining with the long-term desertification process has resulted in massive migration. A World Bank report[3] indicates that the response to the desertification process in Burkina Faso has been a massive migration of almost one million men and women (one-sixth of the national population) which reduced population growth by 40%. Similarly, it has been reported from Niger that the number of children born has been reduced by one–third by migration.

Additional factors mentioned in relation to the rate of population growth in arid lands refer to high mortality rates which do not necessarily take place during drought but rather during the rains after the end of the drought and as consequences of diseases like pneumonia, malaria and tuberculosis.

In general, there would seem to be a connection between the lower rates of natural growth among pastoralists and higher rates of migration. The growth of the pastoral population is slower than overall national population growth. For example, while the population of Kenya was growing at a rate of 3.4% a year, its pastoral population growth was reportedly only 2%. Population increase would therefore be only one cause of desertification among many others. Population dynamics as a cause of desertification should be examined in connection with other factors affecting land-use procedures and the changes induced by the creation of new economic links at national, regional and international levels, which finally result in new patterns of nutrition and new habits and technologies.

The current analysis is that human beings are both the cause and the victims of desertification. Yet most analysis has concentrated on the first aspect. There has been a tendency to overlook the effects of desertification on people and social systems unless a major crisis is given television coverage.

Dryland societies have developed economic and social systems which take into account the constraints and potentialities of their natural environments. Their relationship with the environment is precarious because of the characteristics of the environment and also because of the relatively low technological development which reduces the ability to respond to change and to adopt alternative solutions. These societies tend to adapt to the natural environment rather than to dominate it. Desertification stems from the failure of societies in search of alternative development paths in arid lands. This failure finally destroys society's hold on the natural system. As Eckholm[4] pointed out, people are forced by circumstances to undercut the ecological base of their future welfare in their struggle for survival. The fight against mismanagement of the land can succeed only as part of a more general onslaught against underdevelopment.

The immediate consequence of desertification is to increase the threat to health and well-being.

Lower productivity of the natural system means that the land is no longer capable of sustaining the livelihood of the population. The immediate consequences are a deteriorating nutritional status and increased morbidity and mortality, especially among the more vulnerable groups such as children and the elderly.

Ghana, like other African countries, has reported higher infant mortality in the drylands than in the rest of the country, which is all the more serious as Africa already has the highest rates of child mortality in the world. Above-average mortality has also been reported among young and old people on the Ethiopia–Kenya border. In Brazil, life expectancy in the drylands was 10 years below the national average in 1970 and 14 years below average in 1980, a clear indication that the fight against mortality has been waged mostly outside the drylands. African data show that life expectancy is lower in arid countries than in the rest of the continent. In Sahelian countries, as well as Ethiopia and Somalia, life expectancy at birth is 43 years or less, as against 50 for Africa and 56 for developing countries as a whole. Obviously these indicators do not establish a direct causal effect between aridity and mortality since these countries are also among the least developed in the world. But it does appear that lack of development and a more hostile environment are connected with higher rates of mortality.

The declining productivity of the natural base and its consequences make societies more vulnerable. They have to cope with an extremely uncertain future and they respond to that uncertainty according to their limited capabilities.

For example, for social, cultural and economic reasons, families want at least one son to survive until the average life expectancy age. In the Sahelian countries in the last decade, to have a 95% chance of keeping one such surviving son, a family needed to have five male live births or ten children. In Rajasthan the figure is a little lower — three sons or six children.

The ultimate response to desertification is migration. The consequences of migration and especially its humanitarian aspects should be viewed both from the point of view of the abandoned area and of the receiving area.

In the abandoned area, migration implies the destruction of family patterns. This disrupts population dynamics but also entails the loss of the more innovative individuals. Declining land productivity, increasing labour shortage caused by migration, and the fact that those who stay behind — women, especially — have to devote more time to survival activities (e.g. fetching water and firewood) cause a further fall in agricultural productivity and in overall economic activity. In certain countries such as Mali and Burkina Faso, one-sixth of the population has been uprooted as a result of desertification.

The traditional institutional and social fabric has been destroyed by environmental deterioration and desertification. The precarious balance between people and nature has been upset. In developed countries, a reduction in the agricultural area or the area of cultivable land could be offset by more technological inputs (more intensive culture, greater use of fertilisers). In arid lands the penetration of technology associated with economic schemes ill-suited to the region has contributed to further environmental deterioration and social disruption. In this context, the lack of Research and Development (R & D) for drylands is particularly striking.

Humanitarian problems also arise in the recipient areas. Many people from Burkina Faso and Mali moved to Senegal and Ivory Coast, bringing increasing pressure to bear on poorly equipped services and intensifying marginalization. The same thing happened in Mexico and Brazil. In India, the rapid influx of Hindu settlers into the mainly Sikh state of Punjab from surrounding states affected by desertification helped to inflame Sikh separatist feelings. Refugees from desertification and related disasters often flock to the major cities. In 1974, 20% of Mauritania's population — 250,000 people — had moved to towns and were completely destitute. The slums and shantytowns of Brazilian cities are full of *nordestinos* who left the huge drought-stricken region of Northeast Brazil, an area the size of Western Europe.

Increased urbanization also indirectly contributes to desertification. African and Asian city dwellers cook and heat themselves with charcoal and therefore put pressure on local wood resources. The acacia woodlands which used to surround Khartoum in 1955 have been completely eliminated and only isolated woodlots can be found within 90 km of the city. The woodlands around Nouakchott, in Mauritania, have dwindled as a result of an annual 15.8% growth in urban population. Woodland clearance favours sand-dune encroachment and dust storms, which in turn give rise to additional environmental and health problems.

Increasing urbanization also forces governments to adopt food pricing policies with a distinct urban bias, which penalize rural producers depriving them of all incentive to increase or improve production. Urban political power also results in the concentration of investment in urban areas, with the rural areas affected by desertification left out in the cold.

Roughly 50% of the people most directly threatened by desertification live in the Sahel. Because of the attention given to this problem in the Sahel — and the fact that the best data often come from that region — one tends to forget that other parts of the world are also threatened, not all of them low-lying, sub-tropical areas. Particularly at risk are the Andean areas of South America, Brazil, Mexico, and parts of Western Asia and the Indian Subcontinent.

In the Peruvian Sierra, the cold desert is now rapidly gaining ground. The natural forests which once covered this area have virtually disappeared, and the only remaining wood cover is along steep stream banks and other inaccessible areas. Even this is now being rapidly cut. As a result, rivers are heavily loaded with sediment, water flow is erratic, floods and droughts more common, and nearly all the wildlife — previously an important source of protein — has disappeared.

The area supports about six million people — most of Peru's rural population — who now live in dire poverty.[5] Throughout the region, it is nearly always impossible to meet basic needs for housing, food, drinking water and energy. Annual income ranges from $50 to $200. The cold desert in the Peruvian Sierra means that people now spend one day a week gathering fuelwood; 1.3 million people now use llama- or cow-dung as fuel thus depriving soil of fertiliser, as has already happened in India; houses are heated only when food is being cooked; fuel shortage also means that only an average of 1.3 meals per day are cooked; hot water is no longer used for washing clothes and bathing babies. Similar problems exist in many other parts of the Andes.

Wherever it occurs, desertification affects the poorest among the poor, those who are least able to cope. The victims of desertification are those with little or no land, no political power and tiny incomes. Most depend on their ability to scratch some kind of living from land which is already impoverished. For them, survival depends critically on the crops, animals and trees which provide their basic needs. Hunger and disease arrive quickly in the wake of any external disturbance, such as a drought.

As desertification erodes the few resources to which these people have access, social inequalities are magnified. The poor get poorer — forced, for example, to sell their crops or cattle for almost nothing. In Burkina Faso in 1982, traders were able to buy the harvest at a price of 30 CFA a kilo. At the height of the dry season, seven months later, they sold it for 120 CFA a kilo.

The case of the women of Burkina Faso who have to walk 6 hours three times a week to fetch firewood has been largely used to illustrate the magnitude of the ecological deterioration and desertification of the Ouagadougou hinterland.

Yet little has been said about the fact that this reflects the social disruption caused by desertification. Disruption affects the individual, the family and society as a whole. At the individual level, there are two main implications, one concerning people's nutritional and health situation and a second, their economic activities and social roles.

The scarcity of energy to satisfy basic needs results in additional heavy and time-consuming work, as well as changes in nutritional patterns. More effort goes into producing less food. Families only have one cooked meal a day and a number of traditional staples which take longer to cook — and require more fuel — are often replaced by food of lower energy and protein value. Beans are one staple in the process of being replaced. Things are made worse by the lack of adequate substitutes in drylands. Less nourishing food leads to malnutrition which in turn increases the vulnerability of people to different diseases and finally reduces their productive capacity. The penetration of foreign foods or nutritional habits dependent on irregular supplies of imported commodities is often a further problem.

The diversion of women's activities to the collection of wood and water means a reduction in the productive labour force. This affects agricultural activities — it has been shown that up to 95% of agricultural work in Africa is done by women — food processing (e.g. milk products, salting, grinding etc.), care of domestic animals (goats, sheep), etc. And on top of their economic activities, women take care of the children and the house. The African woman certainly has no time for social and educational activities, let alone rest, during the day.

The reduction of female productive activities is made worse by the emigration of men or complete families, a new cause of decreasing food production. For the family, male migration brings about a structural change as women take on the new role of head of the family. Recent studies show that the trend is increasing in several countries, and that in most cases affected families are living below the line of absolute poverty.

Changes at the individual and family level tend to cause changes in society as a whole which also has to contend with the penetration of new habits and new technology in the form of such schemes as ranching, cash crops etc. For example, the mechanization of activities traditionally undertaken by women leads to their replacement by male workers.

These changes associated with long–term ecological deterioration and the occasional drought or other disasters deal a death blow to the institutional and control mechanisms developed over the centuries or at any rate make them useless. For example, dryland people have developed long-standing mechanisms for livestock management (nomadism), or for coping with such natural hazards as drought, or birth control mechanisms. These mechanisms are destroyed and replaced by new ones which are not accepted by the local population, require special conditions that do not exist or simply do not work in the specific conditions of dryland societies.

Because of the international causes, dynamics and consequences of desertification, any action to cope must also involve international action.

From the purely physical point of view, it is possible to start from the fact that arid and semi-arid areas are particular ecosystems whose limits are not determined by any national boundaries or international agreements. Areas affected by desertification transcend national boundaries. Moreover, the causality link also has an international dimension: actions undertaken in a particular place have natural and socio-economic effects in different and larger areas.

Even if desertification is a local process, it is also caused or accelerated by the interaction of large–scale dynamic processes in the atmosphere and global weather changes with local characteristics, and also by man's action on natural physical processes. An understanding of the overall interaction of the macro-climate with local phenomena is also essential. The scale of the problem is such that it can only be tackled globally.

The international character arises also out of the increasing integration of the different areas of the world and their greater interdependence, which determines how land is used, for what purpose, as well as the type of technology applied.

This is illustrated by the increasing reliance on cash crops

35

at the expense of traditional food crops, in order to supply world markets. This trend has serious effects on drylands. The adoption of agriculture and livestock schemes with the incorporation of technologies often ill-suited to local conditions is another harmful development.

Desertification causes demographic changes which are not restricted to a specific country. Thus, people expelled from their natural habitat by desertification frequently move to less affected neighbouring countries or to states which offer economic or survival alternatives.

Finally, the consequences of desertification that in the short term appear purely local, tend to acquire in the long run a global dimension in terms of increases in atmospheric dust, changes in the hydrological system, climatic change, loss of important genetic varieties, loss of production, and a general reduction of the productive base of society. The increasing vulnerability of those directly affected causes social and political instability, contributes to greater inequality in wealth distribution and delays development.

2. What Has Not Been Done: UNCOD to Now

The only global consideration of the problem took place in the context of UNCOD — the UN Conference on Desertification — and was duly reflected in its 1977 Plan of Action to Combat Desertification. It was not the first word on the problem, and hardly the last, but it does provide a framework in which to analyse what has — and what has not — been done.*

---

*The Plan contained 28 recommendations, which fall under three headings:
(1) *Action to halt desertification:*
    * governments to set up national machinery to assess and monitor desertification, prepare national plans of action, and start action
    * governments to co-operate on wise management of shared resources, especially through six major transnational projects
    * UN agencies, other inter-governmental organizations and non-governmental organizations to participate in the Plan, and consider its recommendations in their programmes;
(2) *Priority measures to include:*
    * sound land-use planning, improved livestock raising, improved rainfed farming techniques, rehabilitation of irrigated lands, environmentally sound management of water resources, protection of existing tree cover, establishment of woodlots, conservation of flora and fauna, and public participation in all measures;
(3) *Improved development planning to:*
    * investigate the social, economic and political factors connected with desertification

Part of the May 1984 12th Governing Council meeting of the UN Environment Programme (UNEP — which is the UN system's lead agency in desertification work) was set aside to assess seven years of anti-desertification efforts. Delegates were told by UNEP[6] that the number of people threatened by severe desertification had increased from 57 million in 1977 to 135 million (rural population only), or from 80 to 230 million (urban and rural populations combined). They were also told that 6 million hectares of land continued to be irretrievably lost through desertification or degraded to desert-like conditions every year, while the amount of the land reduced to zero economic productivity increased from 20 to 21 million hectares per year.

The most affected areas are the developing countries with tropical drylands and especially those belonging to the group of least developed countries, several of which have suffered from the serious international economic situation and from adverse climatic conditions. The increasing land deterioration caused by desertification has had severe effects on agriculture, and therefore on domestic food supplies, on exports, on the balance of payments and on economic growth.

---

* introduce appropriate measures to control population growth
* improve health services
* improve scientific capabilities
* expand awareness of desertification and skills with which to combat it
* assess the economic impacts of settlements and industries on desertification.

Four main priorities were also listed for the period 1977–84. These were:
* the establishment by each government of a national body to assess, monitor and combat desertification, and prepare the national plan
* the organization of regional workshops and seminars to discuss and co-ordinate technical activity on the Plan
* preparatory work for setting up research development and demonstration centres for rainfed cropping, irrigated cropping, livestock and rangeland management and afforestation/revegetation
* organization of the six transnational projects to help link up action and allow nations to pool their experiences.

Between 1969–71 and 1980–82, per capita grain production in the eight Sahel countries fell by 13%, from an average of 198 kg to 172 kg. In the 24 African countries FAO regarded as the 'most seriously affected' by the droughts of 1983–84, the situation is considerably worse, with per capita annual production of grain falling from 150 kg in 1970 to only 100 kg in 1984.[7]

Since the start of the 1970s, food imports to the region have increased at an average rate of 6% per year. In 1981, Sub-Saharan Africa imported more than 12 million tonnes of cereals at a cost of about $2.5 billion. This absorbed more than 27% of total receipts from agricultural, fishery and forestry exports.[8] Among the Sahel countries, only Niger did not ask for food aid during 1983–84. It declared food self-sufficiency in 1981, and increased cereal production by more than 50% between 1974 and 1982, despite a long–term decline of productivity reflected in the fact that the average yield per farmer fell from 500 kg/hectare in 1920 to 350 kg today.[9] The reasons include over-cultivation of marginal land, the bringing into production of yet more marginal land, and government emphasis on the production of cash crops for export.

Concerning the recommendations and priorities of the UNCOD Plan of Action, governments were informed that virtually none of them had been implemented. Only a few governments managed to establish national bodies to co-ordinate national action against desertification.

UNEP comments:[10]

> With few exceptions the planning of desertification projects has been allocated to an existing agency rather than to a separate organization. Of the three national agencies designated by 1982, only one is currently effective, and this is a section within a ministry rather than a government-wide co-ordinating body. This inadequate organizational response is reflected in generally poor progress in national assessments of desertification, despite international and regional assistance, and in a general failure to formulate effective national plans to combat desertification.

Only two countries (Sudan and Afghanistan), of the more than 100 affected by desertification, have prepared National

Plans of Action along the lines recommended by UNCOD.[11] Nine others have prepared draft plans.

Few governments of dryland developing countries have explicitly integrated the problem of desertification into their development planning and, more specifically, in their rural development plans, despite the fact that the majority of their population lives in the countryside. Thus, it is not strange that few of them have made significant progress in their fight against desertification.

Of the six major transnational projects which were recommended, no action has ever been taken on four of them. Only two are said by UNEP to have been started in at least some form.[12] The North African Green Belt is now said to be operating in greatly reduced form in Algeria, Libya and Tunisia. The other project reported to have been started was the joint management of the sandstone aquifer running under Egypt, the Sudan, Libya and Chad. But in August 1984, Libya unilaterally inaugurated an 'artificial river', the source of which is the aquifer itself, to irrigate desert land. Both Egypt and the Sudan have expressed concern that the project will rapidly lower the aquifer's level.

Only two of the regional research and development centres have been set up: the Sahel Institute in Mali and the Regional Agro-Meteorology and Hydrology Centre in Niger.

The special account to finance the Plan, which UNCOD recommended and which was established in March 1979, amounted to only a miniscule $48,524 in January 1984 with only five countries contributing. The special machinery which the UN General Assembly set up to mobilize funds to tackle desertification has managed to raise, in its six years of existence, only $26 million, one quarter of the minimum target figure.

The study requested by the United Nations General Assembly in 1980 estimated the cost of the programme to stop desertification at $4.5 billion *a year* for 20 years, i.e. a total of $90 billion in all. Of this, $48 billion or $2.4 billion a year is required in the form of financial assistance to developing countries. In 1980, the available aid resources for desertification control amounted to $600 million a year, leaving an annual shortfall of $1.8 billion. By comparison, the *annual* cost of damage from desertification in terms of production loss due to land deterioration is estimated at $26 billion.[13]

Knowledge of the extent of desertification, and of the areas at greatest risk, has hardly improved at all. Very little extra has been spent on improved techniques or land-use planning.

In 1977, the Nairobi Plan of Action appeared thorough and responsible. It was generally considered one of the United Nations' better attempts to isolate a global issue, attract international attention, and produce a recipe for repair. However, even in 1977, 20 major donors rejected the original UNCOD plans for setting up new mechanisms to finance the Plan of Action; and in retrospect, the donors' objection to additional funding may have doomed the Plan from the outset.

In 1986, few international experts are surprised that the Plan has not been implemented. Senior FAO officials, for example, comment that in the light of the worsening crisis in Africa, the Plan now appears far too research-oriented. The types of project envisaged in the Plan — many of them long-term, most of them requiring either research or at least considerable background studies — are not appealing either to donors (faced by budgetary cutbacks) or to recipient nations (faced with appalling and far more immediate problems).

With hindsight, it is easy to say that hard-pressed national treasuries are unlikely to respond to requests for finance even to prepare a national plan against desertification when their resources are dwindling and the demands on them increasing.

A retrospective analysis of the Plan of Action reveals that socio-economic aspects, particularly socio-economic constraints, were largely underestimated, while it was over-optimistic about the financial feasibility of the Plan, particularly the availability of funds.

In 1977, desertification appeared to be a major cause of the African crisis. It was logical, therefore, that attention should be focused on it, and attempts made to combat it. The

Plan did maintain that, in the long term, appropriate rural development of affected populations would ease the problem of desertification. But in practice, when anti-desertification programmes are considered at all today, they still tend to emerge as technical fixes in the form of dune stabilization and tree nursery projects. But this approach is bound to fail, because, as noted, desertification is more a symptom of the lack of development. Therefore solutions should be worked out as an integral component of development plans. The aggregation of isolated sectoral projects which ignore the holistic character of the problem is not enough; it does not amount to an actual *plan*.

The lack of development, in particular rural development, in so far as it implies socio-economic disintegration, increasingly unequal wealth distribution and increasing poverty, leads to excessive use of the natural environment, adoption of inappropriate technology, lack of environmental management, and eventually, in arid and semi-arid lands, to increasing desertification.

The development approach emphasizes two elements: its holistic character and the human component. The first is of paramount importance in this case. It has been said that the socio-economic natural balance in arid and semi-arid areas is precarious because of poor development in an extremely demanding environment. In this context, every aspect of the inter-relationship between society and nature plays a critical role and if one of them fails then the whole situation is likely to be severely affected.

The second element is unfortunately frequently forgotten: the *raison d'être* of the fight against desertification is man. Desertification means the destruction of the natural support of life and development. The ultimate goal of actions against desertification is to preserve and enhance such a natural base for the well-being of people.

That is why the absence of this element is startling. Dregne[14] in his evaluation of the progress of the Plan stated: 'The most glaring gap is the near-total absence of projects involving the human factor.'

The human element must be examined from two points of view: with human beings as targets of planned actions and as actors in the desertification drama. This second perspective has two supplementary aspects: human beings as part of a socio-economic system which is at the heart of the problem and at the same time human beings who must act to solve the problem. Again Dregne[15] draws attention to this aspect: 'Unless the socio-economic factors that caused the desertification in the first place are identified and countered, and local people are brought into a decision-making position, combating desertification can only be temporarily, if at all, successful.'

It is not just that social elements have not been taken into account in designing different projects, but that there are no projects dealing with those aspects. Thus even the inadequate sectoral approach appears incomplete. The report of the Executive Director of UNEP indicates that: 'There has been an almost total absence of projects designed to monitor the human condition in desertified lands, to evaluate the socio-economic cost of desertification and to analyse the ecological impacts of population trends.'[16]

But surely a qualitative distinction should be drawn between the *human* dimension and *economic and ecological* considerations. In this context, it is startling to find that there is no project which focuses on people and which tries to understand the social, cultural and religious factors behind their behaviour in relation to desertification.

Worse still, some projects have attempted to change the lifestyle of dryland people without taking into account their needs and goals. A clear example was the project to settle nomadic people which, but for a few exceptions like the NOMADEP project in Ethiopia, finally resulted in increased suffering and environmental deterioration.

Unfortunately, there must be additional negative assessments of the implementation of the Plan of Action. Four–fifths of the proposed investment projects relating to desertification involve preparatory or supportive action and only one–fifth concentrates on corrective action. But even in this category, the emphasis was on infrastructure (road construction, dams or irrigation schemes) or on an increase in dryland production rather than on stopping the deterioration of the natural base. This situation can be

43

illustrated by some recent projects approved by the World Bank, e.g. a $9.4 million project in Gambia to increase groundnut production; a $25.9 million project in Mali for the development of cotton, cereals and groundnuts; a $7.7 million project in Brazil for the development of an irrigation scheme in the North East, etc. While these activities can contribute to the development of the area, if they are not co-ordinated with others they remain isolated efforts which can even make things worse. In short, what is needed is a series of appropriate and mutually reinforcing activities which promote development while at the same time preserving and enhancing its natural base.

Other events also seem to have conspired to make the Plan less effective than it might have been. Its timing could hardly have been worse. By the time UNCOD met, developing countries were already being overtaken by the implications of the international recession — declining funds from donor nations and international agencies, reduced demand and lower prices for agricultural exports, a worsening debt crisis, increasing trade protectionism on the part of developed countries, continued high inflation, harsher loan terms and more self-interested conditions on bilateral aid from donor nations.

The unfortunate occurrence of other events which has made the implementation of the Plan of Action more difficult has been summarized by Mabbutt in the following way:[17]

Climatic conditions in most of the drylands have been unfavourable in the period [since UNCOD] and have accelerated desertification processes whilst hampering combative measures; human and livestock populations have generally continued to increase, but productivity has failed to rise in the face of mounting pressures placed on resources; economic conditions have worsened during major world recession, and terms of trade have become increasingly disadvantageous to Third World countries; investment flows [into anti-desertification projects] have diminished, particularly in the face of the initial low returns to be expected from projects; and in several regions warfare and political strife have not only disrupted the continuity of actions needed to combat desertification, but have worsened the problem itself through the breakdown of livelihood systems and the displacement of populations in the areas most affected.

3. The Developing Countries' Shortcomings

The developing countries can claim that their battle against desertification has been hampered by lack of money. While it is certainly true that globally not enough has been spent on desertification, money has been pouring into selected areas, in particular the Sahel. During 1975–80, the region received at least $7.46 billion in aid, a per capita figure of $40 a year; in Africa as a whole, the figure was only $19 and in the rest of the world even less. Yet the situation in the Sahel has deteriorated steadily.

To assess how much has been spent on activities against desertification is no easy task, especially when trying to isolate the UNCOD and post-UNCOD periods from other actions undertaken in arid and semi-arid lands. Action was already underway before UNCOD. For instance, by 1977, some $500 million had been mobilized for the first Sahelian Development Programme, and a total of $3 billion in new projects had been approved for the first five-year period.

But the institutional machinery within countries as well as the one through which international assistance is channelled have a sectoral character. Specific ministries or agencies deal with each sector of the economy, and institutionalized sectoralization is duly reflected in the budget structure of both donor and recipient countries. There is no ministry for anti-desertification activities, no specific budget provision. Some regional institutions were created in arid and semi-arid lands but normally with different objectives: co-ordination and/or regional development. Thus, for example, the *Comité Permanent Inter-Etats de Lutte contre la Sécheresse dans le Sahel* (CILSS) created in 1973 had, as the name suggests, the purpose of co-ordinating efforts to cope with drought and to promote food self-sufficiency in Sahelian countries. Similarly, the main objective of the United Nations Sudano–Sahelian Office (UNSO), also created in 1973, was to assist the countries of the region in their medium- and long-term rehabilitation from the drought. Hence, the activities considered were to increase food and fertiliser production, pest control and to build adequate infrastructure, mainly roads, to make remote areas more accessible.

The existing institutional machinery is reinforced by the tendency inherited by all disciplines, to offer a sectoral approach to a phenomenon that is fundamentally inter-disciplinary and multi-disciplinary, and therefore, multi-sectoral: each institution or expert thus tends to see the problem only from the restricted perspective of its or his field.

Such an approach is also easier to implement, precisely because of the existence of a sectorally oriented institutional machinery. It was difficult even for specialized donor agencies and assistance organizations to isolate the anti-desertification effort from others.

It is hard to estimate how much of various funding sources has actually gone to projects which can be specifically described as anti-desertification. Patchy figures exist. USAID, for example, estimates that during 1978–83 it spent more than $1 billion on projects 'judged to be within the framework of the UN Plan of Action'.[18] This was 20% of total USAID expenditure on food and agriculture projects over that period.

According to a U.S. report, during 1970–80, the World Bank provided $1.7 billion for 82 desertification-related projects, a figure which was increased by national and other donor contributions to $4.15 billion. Over the same period, FAO spent $294 million on technical assistance against desertification in 34 countries. UNEP spent $14.6 million from 1977 to mid-1983, and UNSO $82.2 million from 1977 to 1981. According to the OECD, all donor countries collectively spent about $1 billion a year on desertification projects (over and above contributions to multilateral organizations which may have eventually gone to anti-desertification work) between 1970 and 1980.

But only about $200 million was spent on actual field projects, although national governments probably contributed at least as much again.

In an evaluation report prepared for UNEP, the author[19] estimated that, worldwide, some $7 billion had been spent on projects with a desertification element during the six years 1978–83, but that no more than $400 million had been spent on activities to control desertification in the field. Most of the rest had gone on 'road construction, buildings, water supplies, research, training courses and meetings'.

Dregne doubted that this money was really laying a sound basis for field activity and pointed out that the money actually being spent in the field was only one–seventh of the total needed to halt desertification; even the total expenditure amounted only to about half of what was needed to implement the Plan.

An evaluation of the financial assistance and aid to areas affected by desertification is easier for the Sudano–Sahelian countries, and in particular for the Sahelian countries, partly because of the existing mechanisms such as UNSO and CILSS, but also because these are the countries most affected by long-term drought.

Berry[20] estimates that the Sudano–Sahelian region was receiving $4.7 billion worth of development assistance per year in 1980 — but that only $150 million of it, about 3.5%, was allocated directly to desertification control.

This amount is more than double that of 1975. Taking inflation into account, however, the real aid contribution in constant (1975) dollars is $3.07 billion. Berry estimates that the total amount needed in the Sahelian region per year for desertification control alone is at least $320 million (1980 dollars). This is probably too little since it does not take into account financial requirements for such activities as sand dune stabilization, protection of woodlands and such supplementary measures as monitoring the desertification process, and providing alternative renewable energy sources to avoid the cutting of fuelwood.

Because of the sectoral character of available data (which are provided for agriculture, rural development, food, education, energy, health, transport, industry, etc., but not for desertification), it is very difficult to identify which part of total development assistance goes to the fight against desertification.

To identify the anti-desertification component or the impact on desertification control, it is necessary to review all projects individually. There is a tendency to assume that financial assistance to agriculture, rural development and forestry is more likely to be in favour of anti-desertification activities than assistance to urban-based activities. It is reported, for instance, that in the Sahelian countries only 24% of aid is directed to agriculture and forestry, less than 40% of all agriculture and forestry projects being rural-based. The rest of the money is spent on urban support activities. Yet in developing countries, the great majority of the population lives in the countryside. Percentages are particularly high in the Sahel, e.g. 91% in Burkina Faso, 87% in Niger, 83% in Mali and 82% in Chad.

According to UNEP's Executive Director:[21]

> Far too much technical and financial assistance has gone to show-piece projects and into measures aimed at appeasing the more politically advantaged urban populations. By comparison, rural populations which tend to lack political clout — especially in the more remote semi–arid regions — are all but ignored. And even when it comes to allotting funds for rural development, agroforestry and other ecologically sound activities are nearly always at the end of the queue.

City dwellers have indeed been the main beneficiaries of

international aid. Urban–rural gaps in terms of access to resources and participation in the distribution of the national product have consistently widened as a result. However, the highly condensed and generalized nature of these comments is potentially misleading.

First of all, it ignores the integral or systematic character of economic activities, and in its inter-relationships an urban-based support project may be directly related to agricultural development and can even produce important effects. The lack of an agricultural label on an aid project does not necessarily mean it does nothing for agriculture. For example, because of the growing demand of city dwellers for fuelwood, great pressure is brought to bear on the hinterland. Action aiming at a rationalization of energy use in urban areas or at providing alternative sources of energy can have important positive effects for land preservation and agricultural development.

Secondly, it tends to support the idea that whatever is rural is good and whatever is urban is bad. Urban development is a reality and politicians and decision-makers have to face that fact. Its dynamics and relationship with the rest of the socio-economic system and the natural environment have to be understood. Furthermore, the history of international development aid is littered with ill-conceived rural projects counter-productive for the natural environment as well as for social development.

While it is true that rural people, and in particular pastoralist and nomadic groups, have little political power, criticizing the urban bias of governments is no answer. What is needed is to give power to rural people and this can be done only by integrated and sustainable development.

Thirdly, some of the projects implicitly regarded as detrimental to rural development (e.g. highways or factories) may contribute significantly to overall socio-economic progress, and stimulate further rural development.

Similarly, the problem of cash crop rather than food crop-oriented financial assistance deserves close scrutiny. The negative environmental and social impact of homogenous cultivation and the shift from food crops to cash crops has already been mentioned.

51

The available evidence shows that most international financial assistance goes to cash crop projects. For the Sahelian countries, some 28% of agricultural aid was spent on cash crops (mainly peanuts and cotton). Of the grand total, only 8% was spent on rainfed food crops, only 5% on livestock raising and only 1.4% on forestry/ecology.[22]

Developing countries are faced with a dilemma: whether to use land resources to increase foreign currency earnings, or to put the production of food crops for home consumption first. Countries have to strike a balance between environmental constraints and development goals both in the short and in the long term. This is what was recommended by the Lagos Plan of Action for the African countries, which stated:[23]

> Research should also be intensified in the area of root crops, tubers and soya beans, and in improvement of production and nutritional values of all food crops; research should also continue in the area of agricultural export products, which bring in not only the foreign exchange needed for development, but also provide raw materials for domestic production.

Often, however, the final decision is based more on such considerations as anticipated return on investment and donors' interests, which both tend to tip the scale in favour of cash crop investment.

Many of the countries directly affected endorse the goal of food self-sufficiency, yet pay scant attention to the kind of rural development which will make that possible.

Some countries have suffered from an overdose of ill-planned aid. This has been followed by a flood of international advisors and development experts who have not always improved matters.

Poor planning and inadequate national support, resulting from over-stretched resources within recipient nations, have increased the rate of project failure.

Recipient Country Priorities

However, the UNCOD Plan of Action involved a great deal

more than specific field projects. It required governments to face up to the problem of desertification, assess its significance, prepare a national plan of action integrated into national development planning, and set up a national body to co-ordinate anti-desertification action.

UNEP's Executive Director states:[24]

> Without coherent national plans and lacking adequate government mechanisms, countries have carried out little of what the Plan of Action proposed regardless of the impact on them being made by desertification. Assessments of the problem have generally not been made nor have national priorities been established.

Dregne was more specific:[25]

> Governments do not see desertification as a high priority item. Rangeland deterioration, accelerated soil erosion, and salinization and water-logging do not command attention until they become crisis items. Lip service is paid to combating desertification but the political will is directed elsewhere. There seems to be little appreciation that a major goal of many developing nations, that of food self-sufficiency, cannot be attained if soil and plant resources are allowed to deteriorate.

It seems that planners and decision-makers actually fail to make the connection between desertification and failure to achieve food self-sufficiency. The fact is that, although many countries have declared food self-sufficiency a national aim, they have done little or nothing about desertification. Evidence of the type of priorities can be gleaned from the analysis of a number of different indicators: levels of domestic spending on agriculture, access of the small farmer to agricultural inputs such as fertilisers, attempts at land reform, and per capita earnings of those employed in agriculture.

Data on domestic expenditure on agriculture in desertification-affected countries is sparse and unreliable. The most serious attempt to assess the situation has been made by FAO.[26] During 1978–82, 13 out of 37 countries for which data were available showed a downward trend in domestic expenditure on agriculture. In seven of them — Argentina, Bolivia, Chile, Colombia, Costa Rica, Gambia and Ghana — the rate of decline was more than 10% per annum. Yet in Gambia, Ghana, Bolivia and Costa Rica, more than half of the population lives in the countryside.

Data are more abundant for the period 1978–81, but the figures are worse. Information is available on 47 countries, and domestic expenditure on agriculture declined in real terms in nearly half of them. The rate of decline was more than 10% in nearly one-quarter of them. The situation was the least satisfactory in Africa, where there was decline in half of the 14 countries studied.

The situation is even more dismal when measured by domestic spending on agriculture per head of agricultural population: in the 17 African countries for which data were available, the average level of spending actually declined by 0.1% between 1978 and 1982.

Table 1
Level and Growth of Public Sector Allocation of Resources to Agriculture per capita, 1978–82 (in $)

Region	Year					Annual Rate of Growth
	1978	1979	1980	1981	1982	(1978–82)
Africa (17)	26.3	28.3	30.1	26.3	22.9	−0.1%
Far East (7)	17.7	22.4	21.8	23.1	24.3	7.3%
Near East (7)	74.0	82.6	84.3	85.2	63.3	1.9%
Latin America (17)	69.8	76.6	83.5	90.7	84.7	3.0%
All regions (48)	47.4	52.5	55.7	57.2	50.9	2.5%

Figures in brackets indicate number of countries for which data were available.

Source: FAO, 1984.[27]

If it is assumed that anti-desertification spending is part of expenditure on agriculture, and that soil conservation and anti-desertification are not among the priorities within agriculture budgets, then the situation appears rather gloomy.

Part of the process towards national food self-sufficiency is providing small farmers with access to agricultural inputs such as credit, fertilisers and improved seeds. In several countries however, the small farmers — even where credit facilities exist — receive a very small proportion of total advances, mainly because the lending agencies maintain a bias in favour of larger farmers in order to minimize administrative costs and risk.

In such a situation small farmers with very limited resources concentrate on productive rather than protective activities, looking for short-term tangible returns, rather than soil preservation, let alone regeneration. Small farmers using marginal land are likely to have a negative impact, leading to soil deterioration and ultimately to desertification.

Another factor is that lending agencies almost never consider anti-desertification or soil conservation among their criteria. Therefore, larger farmers do not receive any incentive from financial organizations and finally do not assign any priority to measures liable to prevent soil deterioration.

The use of fertiliser can be considered as an indicator of efforts to restore the lost bioproductivity of land. Yet the consumption of fertiliser in developing countries is still at very low levels partly because of increasing prices and partly because of the lack of foreign currency. It is even reported that, in some African countries, fertiliser use has actually declined over the past few years. Developing countries covering the greater part of the world account for only about 20% of world consumption of fertiliser in nutrient terms. It should be noted, in addition, that according to FAO more than half the fertiliser goes to export-oriented cash crops.

Land reform is often critical for the success of desertification projects. Such projects are by their nature long-term. It follows that where farmers have only short-term tenure of their land — as is common in Latin America and Asia —

they have little incentive to invest either money or labour in projects from which they may never receive the benefit. In many parts of Africa, land is often owned on a semi-communal basis, and farmers are given the right to crop certain areas by village chiefs. In Burkina Faso, the land is reallocated every few years. Farmers who have no reassurance that they can go on farming the same land far into the future have less incentive to ensure its long-term fertility, and even less to plant on it trees which take more than a decade to mature.

Legal rights concerning trees often discourage tree planting. In some countries, because all forest land is owned by the government, people fear that if they plant trees, ownership of their land will revert to the government. Elsewhere, people who have the right to crop their land may not actually have the right to cut trees and shrubs which grow on it (this is equally the case in the United Kingdom or Switzerland). In parts of the Sahel, farmers are unwilling to grow certain tree species because they are on the forest department's protected list; to crop or prune them, farmers have to go through tedious procedures to prove they planted the trees and own the land — and even then, they must obtain a cutting permit.

Since the World Conference on Agrarian Reform and Rural Development (WCARRD) in 1979, land reform has been as closely monitored as available statistics will allow. However, since WCARRD, 'only five countries have introduced significant policy changes . . . with a view to making land available to the rural poor.'[28] These include Benin, Cape Verde and Zimbabwe. Over the past 15 years, major reforms have been carried out in four African countries — Angola, Ethiopia, Mozambique and Tanzania — which have made the land the collective property of the people, the community or the state. However, FAO notes that, in Africa, 'there have been no drastic changes in policies effectively governing customary land tenure . . . land reform has not usually gone beyond the promulgation of a law vesting all land titles in the Government.'[29]

Lack of progress here has had immediate and serious results on attempts to control desertification. For example, in the Sahel, USAID has actually decreased its funding for forestry projects following an evaluation exercise.[30] The Agency found that its projects were not producing expected results because the local people were not getting the benefits from the trees and were therefore unwilling to protect them.

Pastoralists, who number one in ten of Africa's population, are in an even worse situation. Although the Action Plan called on governments to make every effort to improve conditions for pastoralists, very little has actually been done. In the FAO's view:[31]

> A few countries have tried to provide pastoralism with an institutional backing largely through the creation of pastoralists' associations, but such efforts are rare and are an exception to the general rule of neglect and apathy towards pastoralism. Organizations of large-scale commercial ranch operations have in some cases deprived the pastoralist population of their traditional grazing areas.

Finally, a key indicator of rural development is provided by income levels in the agricultural sector. In developing countries as a whole, there has been some progress; but FAO[32] again notes that the 'agricultural population in a large number of African countries (16 out ot 37) experienced an absolute decline in agricultural income while their counterparts in about two–thirds of the Near East and Far Eastern countries increased incomes by an impressive rate of

Table 2
Average Annual Rates of Growth of per capita GDP and Agricultural Incomes, 1969–81(%)

Region	Per capita GDP	Per capita agricultural income
Africa	0.81	0.13
Far East	3.49	2.82
Near East	6.30	2.88
Latin America	2.81	3.59

Source: FAO, 1984.[33]

Table 3
**Major Determinants of Agricultural Production Decreases,
1975–83, in Sub-Saharan Africa**

Country	Adverse Weather	Political Unrest	Inappropriate Agricultural Policies
Angola	—	2	1
Burkina Faso	1	—	1
Cape Verde	2	—	—
Central African Republic	—	—	2
Chad	2	2	1
Ethiopia	2	2	—
Gambia	1	—	2
Ghana	1	1	2
Guinea	2	—	—
Kenya	1	—	1
Lesotho	2	—	—
Liberia	—	1	2
Madagascar	1	—	1
Mali	2	—	2
Mauritania	2	—	—
Mozambique	2	2	—
Senegal	2	—	2
Sierra Leone	1	—	—
Somalia	2	2	1
Tanzania	1	—	1
Uganda	—	1	1
Zaire	—	—	2
Zambia	2	1	2
TOTAL	29	14	24

Key: 1 = moderate influence
2 = strong influence

Source: adapted from Olive, 1984.[34]

more than 4% per annum.' In five African countries, per capita agricultural income declined at a rate of more than 3% per annum, implying that their level of income nearly halved within a period of 12 years. Among them are

Botswana, Ethiopia, Niger and Zaire — all countries subject to desertification.

Few analysts have so far managed to provide any overall quantitative evaluation of the role of rural and agricultural policies in combating desertification. One indication of the relative importance of the issue is provided by Olive[35] who has compared the role of adverse weather conditions, political unrest and inappropriate agricultural policies in agricultural production decreases in Sub-Saharan Africa (see Table 3).

The Cash Crop Issue

Although agricultural policies vary from country to country, they also differ markedly in terms of the crop itself: cash crops are treated very differently from food crops. Farmers raising cash crops tend to get the limited credit facilities, fertilisers, pesticides, advice and marketing assistance available in most Third World nations. They also tend to get the best land. But, as governments have been emphasizing cash crops to balance their budgets, revenues from these commodities have been falling steadily, encouraging governments to devote even more land to cash crops.

During the colonial period, the peanut was the main cash crop in many Sahel countries. In Senegal, half of all cultivated land is used to grow peanuts. Peanuts have now been supplemented in many areas by cotton. Significantly, cash crop production in the Sahel *increased* steeply during the period of severe drought, while food production slumped. During 1967–72, for example, peanut production in Mali increased by 70% and cotton production by 400%.[36]

The implications of cash crop monoculture for the soil have been examined in Chapter 2. What is important in this chapter is to point out that, because of the need for foreign currency, governments tend to establish measures and incentives for the expansion of cash crop production which have a number of adverse effects.

Increased demand for cash crops has virtually wiped out fallow time and crop rotation systems which proved their worth over decades by both maintaining the land in good

59

condition and producing food crops as well. Typically, peanuts were either grown in rotation with millet, or grown for three years, followed by a six-year fallow period. Crops were also grown in association with acacia tree species, which helped fertilise the soil and provided shade and fodder during the dry season.

The introduction of mechanization had led to the removal of trees from the fields. Expensive community projects to reintroduce acacia trees are now in operation.[37] Meanwhile, soil fertility has declined so much in some areas that the amount of fertiliser needed threatens to make the crop uneconomic. Instead of being encouraged, fallowing is actively discouraged. In Senegal, for instance, a law has been introduced which removes the ownership of land from any farmer who does not plough within a three-year period. (In Tunisia, a law actually grants ownership to farmers who plough up communal grazing land.) Farmers unable to afford sufficient fertiliser are forced to expand cash crop production on to more land in order to maintain their income.

In the late 1970s, three–quarters of Senegal's export earnings came from peanuts and four–fifths of Chad's from cotton. Both governments and large farmers in West Africa have become critically dependent on cash crops to pay for imports and taxes, respectively. This continued concentration of agricultural interest on non-food crops, grown mainly by large farmers, for the specific purpose of earning foreign exchange, has played an important part in increasing the desertification hazard in many countries.

In spite of that, cash cropping is not, of course, intrinsically associated with desertification.

In developing countries, the little room for manoeuvre over the balance of payments and foreign exchange situation has been exacerbated recently by falls in international trade and by commodity pricing structures. The prices received by developing countries for raw materials are now at their lowest levels for 30 years, while many of the imports needed in developing countries have reached all-time price highs. In Africa as a whole, the purchasing power of agricultural exports for imported manufactured goods and crude petroleum in 1982 was only 55% of its value in 1978. Since 1978, the agricultural export prices of all developing countries have been falling in real terms at an annual rate of between 10% and 17%.[38]

However, the lack of any short-term alternative and urgent foreign currency needs tend to increase the cash crop area.

Pricing Policies and Import Controls

The situation with regard to food crops is quite different. Food prices are deliberately kept at artificially low levels in most developing countries in order to placate potentially troublesome urban populations. The farmers get little for their produce, and have small incentive to produce larger surpluses, and no money to invest in improved seeds, tools, fertiliser and irrigation which are badly needed if the goal of food self-sufficiency is ever to be attained. This policy — coupled with the fact that cash crops get more government extension and credit support than food crops — encourages farmers to switch to cash crops, making the official goal of food self-sufficiency even more elusive. By favouring homogenization of culture in arid or semi-arid areas and use of marginal land for food crops, this policy contributes to the desertification process.

Low food price policies would make more sense if they were on a nation-wide basis. They rarely are. State-run grain agencies buy harvests cheap and sell them cheap in the cities. They have little control over sales in the countryside, where trade is dominated by efficient speculators who may buy cheap in the cities and sell dear to the very farmers who were forced to sell cheap in the first place.

As Twose writes,[39] 'In reality, rural populations, lacking political muscle, have been all but ignored by hard-pressed Sahelian governments who look at national figures or regional shortages but seem unable to focus down on the individual family's ability to obtain food at different times of the year.'

Prices are not the only problem. In Tanzania, as in many

developing countries, laws require that cereal surpluses be sold to the national milling company. Officially, collection is made from the villages shortly after harvest. In practice, poor organization, lack of vehicles, spares and fuel, and dirt roads which are frequently impassable to trucks, mean that farmers often have to wait up to a year to sell their produce. Most villages have only traditional stores for grain, and by the time the truck arrives they have either rotted or been eaten by rodents.

Projects to help villagers build modern grain stores have been in operation for several years. Here again, national policies are counterproductive. Because of harsh import restrictions, virtually no materials are available to the villagers to build their stores with. They are therefore forced to make their own bricks. But bricks can be made only after the rains, when sufficient water is available. The rains occur shortly before the harvest, when food supplies are at their lowest. At this time of the year, many of the men are forced to travel to work on the fields of large farmers to earn enough money to pay for food until the harvest. Consequently, there is little or no labour available for brick-making, and progress in erecting storage sheds is slow.[40]

This is but one example of the unexpected implications of national policy on the rural poor. Import restrictions and the protection of foreign exchange are needed in countries with low export potential. Yet they often work to the detriment not only of the few manufacturing industries with export potential but of the rural poor themselves. And if there is nothing available for farmers to buy, there is little reason for them to strive against difficult odds to increase their income.

Such examples emphasize the need for policies which favour the rural farming community. In Africa, few such policies exist. Even FAO is relatively outspoken in its criticism of current policies:[41]

A bias against agriculture generally, and food production in particular, has become built into the socio-economic structure of many African states, and affects such fundamental issues as exchange-rate and taxation policies, relative price levels, and priorities for the development of infrastructure. It is reflected also in the relatively low prestige attached to work in the farm sector. If food production is to find a new vitality, many countries will have to alter profoundly the attitude towards agriculture held not only by planners and politicians but also by the population as a whole.

But it should also be pointed out that to revitalize food production the fundamental resource must be preserved and regenerated, i.e. the soil. Hence policies for agriculture and rural development must explicitly incorporate elements of environmentally sound management and anti-desertification measures.

Food Imports and Food Aid

Meanwhile, most countries afflicted by desertification are dependent on food imports, if they can afford it, and on food aid if they can't (see Table 4). Either way, they enter a vicious circle which it becomes increasingly difficult to break out of. Imported food consumes foreign exchange which might be better spent on agricultural inputs such as fertiliser and seed. And cereal imports in the last 20 years have increased very rapidly in most of the low-income countries, including China and India. Developing countries imported in 1960–61 a total of 20 million tonnes of grain. In 1977–78 the figure was 70 million tonnes and 98 million in 1979. If the trend continues, imports can be expected to reach 120 to 145 million tonnes by 1990. Imports in 1983–84 were expected to be 19% higher than in the previous year; and 22% higher in Africa.

Many developing countries are importing increasing amounts of prestige foods, such as wheat and rice, following the shift in urban demand. But if food tastes change in this way, food self-sufficiency becomes even more elusive, for these crops are often difficult to grow in arid and semi-arid countries, especially where the threat from desertification is high. In 1982, 84 developing countries unable to grow wheat on any significant scale were importing more than 12 million tonnes of it.[42] Increasing demand for such foods means increased imports, which in turn reinforce Western patterns of consumption.

Table 4
**Commercial Cereal Imports and Food Aid: Selected Countries,
1981**

Country	Cereal Imports (kg per capita)	Food Aid (kg per capita)	Food Aid as % of Imports
Afghanistan	59.2	4.6	7.8
Bangladesh	11.9	8.1	68.1
Bhutan	23.0	7.7	33.5
Burkina Faso	11.3	8.1	71.7
Burundi	4.5	2.9	64.4
Chad	3.1	3.1	100.0
Ecuador	36.9	0.5	1.4
Egypt	168.3	43.1	25.6
Ethiopia	6.5	7.1	109.2
India	2.2	0.6	27.3
Kenya	30.7	9.9	32.2
Madagascar	29.8	2.9	9.7
Malawi	18.2	2.7	14.8
Mali	14.8	7.2	49.0
Mauritania	113.8	66.3	58.3
Morocco	132.0	5.7	4.3
Mozambique	29.4	12.4	42.2
Niger	15.6	1.9	12.2
Pakistan	3.6	3.3	91.7
Peru	73.2	6.8	9.3
Senegal	77.6	25.9	33.4
Somalia	98.2	75.0	76.4
Sudan	15.9	10.2	64.2
Tanzania	13.9	12.4	89.2
Uganda	2.9	4.4	151.7
Zaire	18.0	2.6	14.4
Zambia	50.9	14.5	28.5

Source: World Bank, 1983.[43]

International food aid often fuels the change in consumption patterns because the donors mostly give their own surplus products. Usually, food aid neither matches the tastes of the recipient population nor meets their food habits and needs. Thus food aid promotes the change in nutritional habits and the shift away from indigenous foods suited to the local characteristics of soil and climate and to the tastes of the local population. This can have extremely serious implications for the most vulnerable among the local population, such as children suffering from malnutrition: the new type of food can result in the propagation of diarrhoeal diseases and a sharp increase in mortality. Massive aid in the form of milk and sweet bread has been shown to have this type of effect.

As the population gets used to the new foods, measures are taken to stimulate home production of crops unsuited to local conditions. Productivity is low and the soil deteriorates. The need for imported fertilisers and pesticides severely taxes the scarce foreign currency reserves.

Nor is it easy for the rural people themselves to adapt to the new crops and cultivation methods.

When the demand for the new types of food persists after the emergency and cannot be met by local production, imports have to be increased. The fact that food aid is becoming a rather regular practice in several countries affected by desertification means that the local population is more exposed to the new tastes and may finally adopt the new nutritional pattern.

Finally, it should be also considered that aid can serve other purposes in the recipient countries. Just as for donor countries aid can be a good way to get rid of surplus stocks and maintain internal prices, so it helps recipients to alleviate their budgetary problems.

About 70% of the $1.25 billion worth of food aid sent to developing countries is given or sold cheap to governments, who usually sell it in turn and use the proceeds to help balance their budgets. Only about 30% of this food is meant to be distributed free of charge to the poor (only about 10% is meant for disaster relief). Thus relatively little of the food aid sent to the Third World does what the donor public thinks it does, i.e. feed the very poor and the disaster victims.

65

The 70% which recipient governments control can even serve to make the poor poorer, to introduce new tastes and delay agricultural development. Food which governments can make available fairly cheaply to urban citizens or the army can help keep down prices of domestically grown foods. Farmers have little incentive to return to their fields to grow crops they may never be able to sell. Also, it has proved extremely difficult to keep the produce out of the hands of traders intent on making exorbitant profits.

Finally, the massive flow of aid may also run into handling difficulties because of the lack of infrastructure. Food aid has been massively misused in the Sahel,[44] though this is not the place for an extensive analysis. It is enough to quote one recent first-hand report from the field,[45] on Senegal:

> Before the start of the 1984 rainy season, Dakar harbour could no longer cope. With hangars and silos full to the brim, grain simply spilled over the harbour walls, whereas hundreds of tons of rice, carelessly stored in the open or on the floor, simply rotted away. Broken rice . . . unfit for human consumption was auctioned off to the highest bidder. Clever traders, . . . sect leaders with excellent connections with top decision-makers, make quick profits from this, just as they were reported to profit from tax-free food imports from the Ivory Coast and from a 2,000-ton emergency animal feed programme, financed by Switzerland, that had originally been meant for needy cattle breeders in the hardest-hit Sahelian region in the country.

This illustrates the fact that aid not only often has no positive effect on rural development and desertification control, but does not even alleviate the food problem in arid and semi-arid areas.

4. The Donors' Failures

Some of the blame for the overall failure to cope with desertification rests with those who have expressed the desire to finance and assist such work.

Clearly, they have not provided sufficient funds. But even those funds which were made available have not always been used effectively. Donors have opted too often for the easy way out: the financing of the simpler projects — often those with possibilities of procurement of goods and services from the donor country — rather than the more difficult ones for which there is greater need. They have failed to take proper heed of recurrent costs in their projects, with the result that years of work have later proved useless. They have tended to finance individual projects without examining the details of the programme in which they were situated, with the result that promising projects never fulfilled that promise. And they have consistently poured more aid into relatively rich countries rather than support those who need it most — the rural poor in the arid and semi-arid regions of the world.

The resources needed to combat desertification can be channelled through different mechanisms and it is from this point of view that desertification should be analysed since each mechanism pursues different objectives and follows different courses. This type of action or mechanism is summarized as follows:

- aid
- economic and technical co-operation

- technical assistance
- contribution to the Plan of Action to combat desertification

Aid can be implemented bilaterally or by multilateral arrangement. Strictly speaking, aid is of a short-term character and fails to deal with the causes of the phenomenon. It is a compensatory type of action which does not attempt to change the structural causes of the phenomenon. It alleviates pressure in the short term, but if the problem is to be solved, then other measures should be taken to eliminate the causes.

The other three types of action can be short-term or long-term. What is important is to have the appropriate mix, i.e. action to relieve short-term, immediate pressure but also action to tackle the structural causes of the problem.

A second aspect refers to the sectoral or subsectoral classification of the resources. The classification that lists everything under 'Agricultural Aid' does not show how much has been channelled to the fight against desertification. In other words, the analysis of the changes in the flow of international resources under the title of Agricultural Aid can be misleading.

An exhaustive analysis of this type is beyond the scope of the present Report which has to rely on available secondary data.

The Quantity of Aid

Lack of financial resources has often been mentioned as one of the main reasons for failure to carry out the UNCOD Plan of Action. The United Nations Administrative Committee on Co-ordination (ACC), for example, reported that insufficient financing was 'seriously limiting the efforts of the United Nations system to implement the Plan of Action and that there was an urgent need for external sources to increase their assistance to anti-desertification projects.'

As already mentioned, desertification does not appear as a

separate item in the budgets of most bilateral and multilateral donors. This makes it difficult to analyse the funding situation. One approach is to attempt a breakdown of external aid to agriculture. This is not entirely satisfactory, for although in arid and semi-arid regions much agricultural aid is related to anti-desertification work, much of it also goes to cash-cropping schemes and poorly designed and executed irrigation projects, both of which can be part of the problem rather than part of the solution. For instance, new irrigation schemes can cost as much as $17,000 per hectare, and in the Sahel one–tenth of all aid goes to irrigation. Yet during the early 1980s, for every new hectare of land brought under irrigated cultivation, another irrigated hectare went out of cultivation because bad design and bad management had led to water-logging and salinization.

During the 1970s, external aid for agriculture increased sharply as a percentage of total aid. The terms of aid also improved, with a substantial increase in concessional commitments and a small decline in non-concessional ones (see Table 5).

From Table 5 it is clear that multilateral organizations devote a much higher proportion of their commitments to agriculture (33%) than bilateral donors (11%). Some 57% of bilateral concessional assistance to agriculture comes from three countries (the United States, Japan, and the Federal Republic of Germany); if the Netherlands, France and Canada are included, more than 80% comes from just six countries.[46] The United Nations Meeting on the Least Developed Countries held in Paris in 1981 tried to rectify the situation, and most donors at the meeting agreed to increase the share of agricultural aid in the poorest countries.

However, the proportion of aid going to agriculture — which is likely to have some relevance to the problem of desertification — has been stagnating since the late 1970s. According to FAO:[47]

Recent assistance levels fall far short of what is believed to give agricultural development an adequate boost — only 45% of the

69

Table 5
Commitments to Agriculture in relation to Total Commitments to All Sectors, 1974–81

	Growth in Commitments to Agriculture	*Growth in Commitments to All Sectors*	*Agriculture as Share of Total Commitments to All Sectors*	
	1974/5–1980/1 (% p.a.)	*1974/5–1980/1 (% p.a.)*	*1974/5 %*	*1980/1 %*
Concessional	8.6	4.2	18	23
DAC	7.6	3.2	13	17
Multilateral	10.0	7.8	36	41
Non-concessional	6.1	6.8	13	12
DAC	12.2	6.2	2	2
Multilateral	5.5	7.8	31	27
Total	7.7	5.4	16	18
DAC	8.0	4.4	9	11
Multilateral	7.6	7.8	33	33

Table excludes OPEC bilateral and multilateral commitments.
DAC is the Development Assistance Committee of the OECD.
Source: FAO, 1984.[48]

need, according to one FAO study. Further analysis suggests that assistance for agriculture would need progressively to increase by at least 11% a year in real terms in order for developing countries to double agricultural production within 20 years. Moreover, there are trends for the assistance that is provided to be less concessional and for there to be longer delays in loan disbursements.

In 1981, partly as a result of a worldwide economic recession, official commitments of external aid for agriculture fell by 7.5% — the first fall for many years. The decline was largely due to a 15% reduction in bilateral aid, which fell for the second consecutive year. OPEC aid was cut back particularly sharply as a result of declining oil prices. Oil–

importing developing countries suffer whichever way the oil pendulum swings. In the early 1970s their needs for foreign exchange rapidly increased when the price of oil quadrupled. Five years later, their levels of 'oil aid' fell as oil prices stagnated and declined.

It is difficult to assess what might have been done if bilateral aid had continued to expand. The point can at least be illustrated by one example. FAO's Food Security Assistance Scheme has been helping to provide warehouses for grain storage; these provide an emergency supply for times of need, and help to stabilize and control grain prices. In Mali, Niger and Burkina Faso, a total of 73,500 tonnes of storage have already been provided and 9,500 tonnes have been provided for Cape Verde. But, as of late 1983, FAO had $200 million worth of grain storage projects in 15 countries still unfunded. Gaps such as these take on huge significance during times of emergency such as those now threatening much of the Sahel again.

Multilateral aid also suffered from the recession. For example, the World Bank's 'soft loan' division, the International Development Association (IDA), had to reduce its commitments to all sectors from $3.5 billion in fiscal 1981 to $2.7 billion in 1982. The United Nations Development Programme was even more severely affected by declining contributions. In 1982, it announced that it could authorize budget expenditures at only 55% of the level originally planned for the period 1982–86. One direct result of this was to reduce the number of FAO field experts working on UNDP projects from 1,313 in 1981 to 1,037 in 1982. In fact, at this level, FAO had only about two–thirds the number of UNDP-supported field experts of six years previously (in 1974).[49]

This bodes ill for the future. UNDP is a major funding source for United Nations specialized agencies such as UNESCO and FAO — in fact, it provides about half of the external funds used in FAO field projects, and in the past provided substantially more. Many of these projects are essentially pilot studies and demonstrations, designed primarily to develop effective techniques. When successful, they can lead to major investment projects which are typically funded by institutions such as the World Bank and the regional banks. These are the projects which could begin to stop desertification. There is thus a double threat to the future of desertification control: seed money from UNDP is hard to come by, and this is inevitably reducing the number of investment projects which can follow up on technical successes. And the banks themselves are short of the funds which are needed to support investment projects. The second problem comes at a critical time, because many pilot projects have now evolved successful schemes — particularly, for example, in community forestry — and the time is ripe for major investment. It may be slow to materialize.

Also, organizations providing non-concessional aid, such as the World Bank and the regional development banks, may have a hard time justifying investment in anti-desertification work, because the work takes such a long time and the returns are often uncertain. This can be an especially important consideration if the focus of the project in question is to improve a nation's food self-sufficiency. In countries where food prices are maintained at low levels, these projects may never pay for themselves. Thus, the banks are under pressure, for financial reasons, to invest in other areas.

The Focus of Aid

While the recession played an important role in halting the expansion of agricultural aid, other issues were also involved. For example, agricultural projects in general — and certainly anti-desertification projects in particular — tend to be more difficult to implement than projects in other sectors, and donors tend to shy away from them, particularly in periods of declining aid. An attitude which flies directly in the face of the maxim that aid should be directed where there is most need. As FAO comments,[50] '. . . it is unthinkable that aid donors should be deterred by such problems from contributing to the sector which at least for the foreseeable future holds the key to economic and social development in the countries in greatest need of aid. The difficulties need to be confronted, not shirked.'

One example of the way this works is the tendency for donors to use their aid to finance the supply of agricultural inputs, which avoids most of the difficulties associated with agricultural projects in general, and also has the advantage, from the donors' point of view, of creating a demand for their own productive systems. This tendency, therefore, contributes to maintaining the level of economic activity in donor countries — an element that can be of great importance in periods of economic recession. How the inputs are then used remains an open question. Nor does aid of this kind do anything to encourage recipient countries to produce their own agricultural inputs more cheaply or more efficiently.

Agricultural projects — and particularly those connected with desertification — also tend to have a higher proportion of local and recurrent costs than projects in other sectors. The chances of success in their implementation also depend critically on the way individual projects are related to programme development in general. For instance, tree nurseries for reforestation projects may be pointless when there is no system or funding for growing the trees planted in the right places and cared for and protected while they grow. Failure to co-ordinate, integrate and follow up desertification projects has been a major cause of project failure. The WCARRD Plan of Action addressed these and other related issues in 1979:[51]

> In the least developed and most seriously affected countries in particular, donors should be ready to finance: (a) local and foreign capital exchange costs, as appropriate; (b) recurrent as well as capital expenditures; and (c) an increasing share of programme and sectoral supports as compared to the project approach.

The issue of recurrent costs is important in desertification control and land recovery, which by its nature is a long-term activity. Seeds may be sown, pasture rested, tree seedlings planted, and sand dunes stabilized. But unless projects to organize such activities also ensure that provision is made for the future, the work is wasted. Because donors have not examined in sufficient detail the issue of recurrent costs, a number of desertification projects have floundered: stabilized sand dunes have become unstabilized, forestry plantations have been left untended, and reclaimed cropland has reverted to scrub. As Anne de Lattre of the Club de Sahel puts it:[52]

> New projects generate very heavy recurrent budget costs, which cannot be met, and so the project deteriorates. Phase 2 and phase 3 of the project then have to be rehabilitation, not expansion. Since 1976, there has been a 355% increase in real aid flows to the Sahel. But there is actually massive disinvestment taking place, because of those rehabilitation costs.

Donors have often also ignored the programme implications of their projects. For example, it is easier to mount a project aimed at improving subsistence agriculture techniques in an arid region than it is to assist a government in instituting new pricing policies. Yet the former may be useless without the latter, because the farmer has little incentive to adopt the new practices unless he can get a reasonable price for his crop. Mistakes of this kind are now rarer among multilateral agencies but still common with bilateral donors, who often do not know enough about agricultural constraints in drylands.

Many of the community forestry programmes in the Sahel have come unstuck for this reason. As already mentioned, land reform is often an essential prerequisite to forestry schemes if local people are to identify with, and benefit from, the tree crop. In one project in Niger, seedlings were actually destroyed by local people because they had been planted against their will on traditional grazing grounds.[53]

There remains one overriding reason why funds for desertification control have not been forthcoming, and have not been sensibly directed into the areas where the need is greatest; donors still tend to direct their agricultural aid at areas with low poverty rather than those with high poverty (see Table 6).

Unfortunately high poverty areas are precisely those worst affected by desertification. A recent study[54] by the Italian *Dipartimento per la Cooperazione* on international aid to Sahelian countries shows that, despite concentration

Table 6
External Aid Commitments to Agriculture, 1974–81

Countries by Poverty Group	Aid as a % of Agricultural GDP %	Aid per capita of Agricultural Population ($) $
High poverty	5.9	8.4
Medium poverty	4.9	9.5
Low poverty	8.8	19.5

Source: FAO, 1984.[55]

of international aid on irrigation development schemes in the area as a whole, in the three countries with the lowest GNP, international aid goes to rural development and water supply projects whereas, in the countries with higher GNP, it goes to specific areas like livestock or irrigation schemes.

No doubt the returns are safer, the investment more easily justified. In the Sudan, for example, investment in the expansion of irrigated farming along the Nile looks like a much better prospect, and donors are likely to favour it. But such a priority cannot serve well the causes of the fight against desertification, whatever its apparent economic justification.

Specific examples of desertification-affected countries which receive small amounts of agricultural aid per head of agricultural population include Bangladesh ($2.8), Brazil ($4.1), Ethiopia ($1.6) and India ($1.4). By contrast, countries such as Argentina, Costa Rica, Honduras, Nicaragua and Panama — which are not affected by this problem — receive more than $20 of aid per head of agricultural population. It is also significant that while figures for Bangladesh, Brazil and India improved greatly in 1980–81 compared with the average for 1974–81 (increases of 59%, 31% and 36% respectively), the situation in Ethiopia failed to show the slightest improvement. These figures should be analysed more carefully in order to avoid important conceptual errors. For example, Bangladesh has a very large rural population and high population density. Its

75

agriculture is labour intensive and mainly geared to local markets. In contrast, Argentina's smaller population is predominantly urban, its population density is rather low, agricultural production is more mechanized requiring a relatively low labour input, and production is oriented mainly to international markets.

India is also mainly a rural country with a population about 20 times that of Argentina and its agricultural productive structure more diversified and characterized by the co-existence of different systems.

The conclusion is inescapable: donors tend to put their money where the action is, not where it should be.

The problem of Ethiopia raises the issue of political allegiance. Ethiopia is aligned with the Soviet Union, which gives it very little of what Western nations refer to as official development aid. But because of that alliance, Western nations also tend to give Ethiopia relatively little considering the needs of the country. Africa receives on average about $19 aid per head, Ethiopia a mere $6. In 1984, about half the United States' total economic aid for Sub-Saharan Africa went to five close allies: Kenya, Liberia, Somalia, Sudan and Zaire.

An analysis of capital commitments over the years to agriculture in developing countries, and to various sectors within them, provides a key to the effect the Plan of Action has had on desertification spending. Had the Plan been effective in increasing funds and altering priorities, changes should be apparent in the overall pattern of sector allocation, and in particular within desertification-affected countries. The funds involved should have been large enough to effect major changes of this type. The cost of the Plan in external assistance was estimated at $2.4 billion a year. Over the two year period 1980–81, total external commitments to agriculture were in the region of $10 billion annually.

The figures in Table 7 provide no convincing evidence that the Plan has had any major effect on the pattern of spending within agriculture. On the contrary, in the one area where an increase would be expected — land and water development — there was a 2% decline. The proportion of spending on

Table 7
Capital Commitments to Agriculture, 1974–75 and 1980–81

Sector	1974–75 (%)	1980–81 (%)
Land and water development	20	18
Research, training and extension	1	4
Inputs	3	5
Manufacture of inputs	18	6
Agricultural services	7	10
Crop production	4	6
Livestock	5	3
Fisheries	2	3
Forestry	2	2
Unallocated	12	12
Agro-industries	5	6
Rural development and infrastructure	17	21
Regional and river development	3	4

Source: FAO, 1984.[56]

livestock and forestry also declined. It is possible that some spending on desertification is concealed within the 4% rise in the rural development and infrastructure sector, the 3% rise in research, training and extension, and even the 2% rise in crop production. Possible but improbable, as is shown by a more detailed analysis of similar figures which compare the situation in desertification–affected countries — for convenience sake, those in the Sudano–Sahelian region will be used — with the pattern in Africa as a whole, other regions and developing countries as a bloc (see Table 8).

The figures in Table 8 are more revealing; they also highlight a few instances of concerted action in a few nations. In Cape Verde, for example, donors channelled their efforts to improve land-use planning and to a large-scale reforestation programme, aimed at planting one million trees a year.[57] Chad devoted nearly three–quarters of its pitifully small volume of agricultural aid — the lowest level of aid within the Sudano–Sahelian region — to crop

Table 8
Percentage of Capital Commitments to Selected Areas of Agriculture, 1980–81, by Selected Countries and by Region

Country	Land and Water	Inputs	Services
Sudano–Sahelian Countries			
Benin	—	0.6	—
Burkina Faso	2.0	1.7	3.5
Cameroon	3.5	0.6	—
Cape Verde	22.1	0.6	4.6
Chad	—	—	—
Djibouti	2.8	—	—
Ethiopia	1.2	—	4.1
Gambia	19.0	26.0	—
Guinea	—	—	—
Guinea-Bissau	3.0	—	14.0
Kenya	3.1	1.8	19.0
Mali	3.8	0.6	1.1
Mauritania	75.1	0.6	3.3
Niger	1.0	1.5	—
Nigeria	16.9	0.3	—
Senegal	3.8	6.2	1.0
Somalia	24.0	0.5	14.9
Sudan	37.2	14.3	2.3
Uganda	—	3.9	0.6
Sudano–Sahelian Region	12.6	3.6	4.3
Africa	8.4	3.4	6.5
Asia and Pacific	23.9	10.0	7.4
Latin America	13.2	0.1	18.0
Near East	22.6	5.5	7.8
Europe	28.7	0.1	13.1
All Countries	18	5	10

Source: figures from FAO.[58]

Crops	Livestock	Forests	Rural Development	Other	TOTAL ($ million)
1.0	—	5.6	92.7	0.1	24.8
13.9	1.3	16.7	38.0	22.9	75.3
38.7	12.4	0.2	38.3	6.3	91.2
—	1.0	27.8	2.6	41.3	15.0
70.3	—	—	25.1	4.6	7.8
1.4	78.5	—	—	41.3	15.0
8.5	—	8.6	22.3	55.3	55.1
0.4	—	—	23.2	31.4	10.8
—	34.4	—	48.9	16.7	24.7
12.7	2.0	—	44.6	23.7	14.4
1.8	1.5	0.2	23.8	48.8	133.5
23.4	7.6	10.4	19.8	33.3	59.8
—	1.3	—	—	19.7	7.5
8.5	6.2	1.4	50.8	30.6	59.7
—	—	—	—	82.8	235.8
12.6	3.9	5.4	17.2	49.9	119.4
7.5	3.0	3.4	6.4	40.3	96.3
4.6	0.1	3.8	8.6	29.1	181.1
38.7	14.2	—	12.6	30.0	48.3
10.2	3.9	3.7	19.4	42.5	1,264.0
13.1	3.5	2.8	23.7	38.6	2,433.1
5.3	1.5	1.4	13.8	36.7	4,359.3
1.2	1.6	3.7	0.9	37.4	2,230.4
6.7	3.7	0.9	14.8	38.0	709.7
5.8	9.3	8.2	—	34.8	405.6
6	3	2	21	35	10.138.0

production. In contrast, Mauritania, with equally little aid, was devoting most of it to land and water conservation projects. Benin was planning to spend nearly all its agricultural aid on rural development, in keeping with its aggressive land reform policies. Niger was the only other country to devote more than half its aid to rural development, a result of its determined policy to increase food production and raise the standard of living of small farmers. Land and water figures for Somalia and Sudan were also relatively high; both countries have attempted to make national desertification plans and set up desertification units.

A comparison of figures for the Sudano–Sahelian region with those for the whole of Africa reveals that a higher proportion of aid is being spent in the affected region on land and water projects than in the continent as a whole. Proportionally more money is being spent on forestry in the region (3.7% as against 2.8%). However, the proportion going to livestock is not significantly higher and the proportion spent on crops is actually significantly lower in the desertification-affected countries than in the continent as a whole. Perhaps the most striking fact is how small a percentage of agricultural aid is spent on crops (10.2%), livestock (3.9%) and forestry (3.7%).

Obviously, it is impossible to decide whether donors or recipients are most responsible for the priorities reflected in these figures. But it is clear that donors are not getting their money into the desertified countrysides of the poor nations' drylands.

Table 8 — which has not been published elsewhere and which is based on FAO computerized data on agricultural aid to every nation in the world — provides a clear summary of desertification action in the early 1980s. The picture that emerges from it confirms the general impression. Country figures reveal isolated pockets of action where substantial amounts of agricultural aid have been directed towards specific desertification-related goals — for example, forestry in Cape Verde, rural development in Niger, anti-desertification planning in Somalia and Sudan.

But a few pockets of action do not add up to a major

international or even regional programme. If the figures are analysed in terms of larger geographical areas, these pockets of action become less significant and eventually disappear from the picture altogether. Thus figures for the Sudano–Sahelian region reveal some differences from figures for Africa as a whole, and even from the global figures. But when the global figures are analysed over time (Table 7), it is clear that there has been no significant redirection of global agricultural aid towards desertification-related activities. The co-ordinated international offensive against desertification has simply never materialized, and donors have not responded in any significant way to the calls to devote more resources to desertification.

For example, Canadian international development aid to the Sudano–Sahelian countries rose from 4.6% of total CIDA aid to developing countries in 1978–79 (out of a total amount of US$53 million) to about 9.4% of the total amount of US$139 million in 1981–82. But out of this percentage less than 1% was directed to anti-desertification activities.

The Conditions of Aid

According to FAO: 'Conditions of aid have been deteriorating. Some bilateral programmes have hardened their loan terms, bringing them closer to commercial borrowing. There has also been an increase in the proportion of aid which is tied to the procurement of goods and services in the donor country, even if they can be obtained elsewhere at lower cost; this tends to lower the real value of aid.'[59]

For instance, external concessional assistance to agriculture fell by 6.9% over 1980–81 while non-concessional assistance increased by 21.4%.[60] This has undoubtedly made life harder for desertification-affected countries. The high interest rates which prevailed in the 1970s and 1980s had already forced developing countries into an impossible strait-jacket. What they needed to pay, to service their loans, quickly became exorbitant in terms of their declining incomes, which derived mostly from the sale of agricultural commodities of decreasing value. 'For the first time, in 1983

81

developing countries disbursed more to service their medium-long-term debts than they received. According to a recent report of the World Bank, the net outflows from these countries reached in 1983 the unprecedented level of $11 billion.'[61]

The fact that conditions of aid are hardening has other implications for anti-desertification work. Bilateral donors now require more feedback from their aid in terms of contracts for home-based industries or employment of their nationals on projects in developing countries. Italy, for example, is currently entering the bilateral field in a big way, with specific contributions for food production and rural development in the Sahel. But it is also insisting on substantial sales of its own equipment as part of its packages, even though heavy mechanization may be inappropriate in desertified countries. And, in general, this means that donors shy away from desertification-related projects, which rarely contain any significant kick-back for the donors; they concentrate rather on projects which may provide valuable returns — for example, building and road construction, and the setting up of industrial plants.

Similarly, agricultural aid is also often unwisely tied to cash crop production. For example, under the first 1975 EEC Lomé Convention, 40% of rural development funds went to the development of crops for export.

The Research Gaps

One of the causes of desertification is the pressure to expand agriculture in marginal land, thus accelerating soil deterioration. This pressure is particularly strong in Africa. The joint report by the Club du Sahel and CILSS stated: 'Rainfed cereals production . . . has continued to develop by extending cultivated areas (instead of by intensification of production).'[62]

This development is frequently associated with the technological gap between Africa and other regions and the idea that desertification is an exclusively African phenomenon. The hasty conclusion is that the reason is that there is no Green Revolution in Africa and that there is no attempt by the international research community to focus attention on the crops that Africa grows. But the assertion is only partly false.

The expansion of agricultural land into marginal areas has occurred not only in Africa but also in Green Revolution territory, i.e. in Latin America and Asia where agriculture has generally followed during the last ten years a process of intensification. Thus the absence of a Green Revolution is not necessarily a reason for expansion into marginal areas.

The problem should be examined from two different perspectives: first, the type of research and technological development and implementation likely to reduce the pressure of agriculture on desertification–prone areas; and secondly, the type of research and technological development necessary for the optimization of the biomass of arid and semi-arid areas and for desertification control.

The staple crops of African drylands are different from those of other continents. Millet and sorghum are the two main staples. Cassava, though low in protein, is popular as it is both drought resistant and requires relatively little labour. In the wetter regions a number of other roots and tubers (yams, etc.) play an important part in the diet (roots and tubers supply an estimated 20% of calories consumed in Africa).

The World Bank[63] pointed out that: 'No major breakthrough has been achieved in genetic improvement of rainfed millet and sorghum, which account for 80% of the cultivated land in the Sahel and other areas of low rainfall.' Instead, work has concentrated on the more common cereals — particularly rice, wheat and maize — which are consumed by more than 3.5 billion people in more than 80 different countries. Millet and sorghum are the staple foods of 13 countries with a combined population of only about 200 million people.[64]

In this context a distinction must be drawn between lack of technological development and the low productivity of certain areas or crops because of poor application of new scientific development. International financial resources for scientific and technological development go to those areas and products most favoured by international markets. Thus some types of grain, especially wheat, are in high demand on world markets not only to feed the human but also the animal population. In 1975–77, 493 million tonnes of grain were used to feed cattle in developed countries whereas developing countries, with much larger human populations, consumed 538 million tonnes.

Sorghum and millet are typical cereals of semi-arid tropical areas. Africa's share of world sorghum production is only 14% whereas its share of sorghum cultivated area is 32%. With the scientific and technological development of the past 20 years or more, yields of hybrid sorghum are now as high as 8 to 10 tonnes per hectare in the United States, while yields of ICRISAT African varieties range between 1,970 and 7,753 kilos per hectare. But the average yield in developing countries is still only 960 kg/ha and as low as 700 kg/ha in Sub-Saharan Africa.

This does not mean that massive distribution of genetically improved seeds is necessarily a solution. The problem is far more complex: adaptation to different environmental conditions and varying tastes also have to be taken into account. Each variety will have to contend with local pests, diseases, soil and moisture conditions, weeds, etc.

But the main incentive for technological innovation is that of quick returns in monetary terms. And as Dr. Swaminathan pointed out, 'the terrible irony is that wherever these crops are feed crops, they are improving, but in those places where they are food crops, they are stagnating'.[65]

The chance to increase the production and incomes of millet and sorghum farmers has therefore been missed. Significantly, during the 1970s millet production fell in four, and sorghum production in five, of the largest producing nations south of the Sahara.[66]

The same is true for roots and tubers, for which technological development has been slower, precisely because those staples are of no interest to donor countries. But production could be considerably increased. The current yield of cassava is between 15 and 20 tonnes per hectare, whereas the potential yield is put at 60 to 100 tonnes per hectare.

Technological progress does not just mean improving the seeds. The success of improved varieties depends on the improvement of such additional factors as fertilisers, pesticides, water development, etc. For example, the importance of pest control in developing countries and specially in tropical countries can scarcely be over-emphasized. In tropical areas crops are confronted with a larger variety of pests and diseases than in temperate zones. There are 54 rice diseases in temperate zones but 500 to 600 in the tropics; for maize, the figures are 85 and 125 and for beans 52 and 250–280. The importance of Research and Development (R & D) in this field for tropical agriculture is therefore considerable.

Finally, the success of any technological development depends on many other factors such as training activities, adequate extension services and efficient marketing.

The second aspect mentioned is the development of science and technology for arid and semi-arid areas. In this case, very scant activities have been developed by the inter-national community. A project proposed to UNEP in 1978 for developing technology to understand the physiology, and for use in management, of the biomass in arid and semi-arid areas was rejected as a zero priority. Curiously enough, a little later the University of Arizona initiated a project similar to the one proposed to UNEP. In this case the motivation was clear: the need to know more about a particular plant inhabiting arid areas — the guayule — not for the development of these areas but rather because it offers an important substitute to *hevea braciliensis* in the production of natural rubber. Although guayule has been used for more than 70 years, almost nothing is known about its physiology, adaptation to different types of soil, require-ments for optimal production, etc.

Similar if not greater difficulties are encountered in the R & D oriented to understanding such unglamorous plants as the neem tree, tamarugo or even acacia. In more general terms, similar deficiencies are noted in the development of technology for desertification control. Even in the few stimulating projects undertaken it has been noted that 'technologies pursued have not been specially innovative.'[67]

85

Institutes for R & D have been created in developing countries, among them IRRI, CIMMYT, the International Institute for Tropical Agriculture, etc. However, these centres follow the lines of agricultural research institutes in developed countries, and they are heavily dependent on them for staff training, basic scientific inputs, etc. Research methods copy those of developed countries and, more importantly, priorities are defined not according to regional priorities but rather by the objectives and conditions of donor countries.

'Local people are not sufficiently qualified; governments will never spend the foreign exchange on purchasing the right equipment; there are no spares, no transport and no petrol.' This type of argument is used as a pretext to justify international attitudes concerning science and technology, a field over which a handful of developed countries are determined to keep control. Financial resources for science and technology development in developing countries are actually diminishing. Moreover, as the World Bank indicated:[68]

Research financed by donors has produced some useful results, but the overall record is mixed. Although some competition in ideas and research strategy is healthy, excessive duplication of effort and conflicting focus among donors have caused problems. By contrast, in the 1960s, successful research in Africa mainly resulted from work promoted by or intended for users (maize research in Southern Africa, tea research in Kenya, for example).

The World Bank went on to argue:[69]

As a result research outputs have not been adequately disseminated; local researchers are often underemployed because programmes lack focus, continuity and coherence; research management is weak and its status low, and what is more important is that researchers are isolated from farmers and extension workers, so nobody can see the direct relevance of research.

This segregation between the research and productive sectors is one of the main problems in developing countries.

At the same time, it helps transnational corporations maintain control over the productive sector of developing countries and perpetuate the South's technological dependence.

On the other hand, a recent report indicates that approximately one–third of all developing countries have virtually no agricultural R & D infrastructure or extension services. These countries are scattered throughout the Sahel, Sub-Saharan Africa, the Caribbean, Central America and the South Pacific. It is not just that they are below a critical threshold but they suffer from an almost total absence of any relevant infrastructure.

A great deal more effort is needed in this area, particularly if regional efforts are to be substantially strengthened and research expenditure doubled over the 1980–90 decade, as the World Bank recommends. As the Bank points out, 'the adaptation of existing technology will not by itself be enough, especially in the dry areas. Major research is needed on new crop varieties, techniques for soil moisture conservation, land use, livestock diseases and systems, and agroforestry.' These are exactly the areas for which the UNCOD Plan of Action recommended regional research and development centres — centres which are still on the waiting list of UNCOD Projects.

5. The Failures of the Implementing Agencies

Although virtually all governments, multilateral institutions, development banks and non-governmental organizations in the environment/development field claim to see desertification as a major threat to the well-being of the planet, the issue of desertification has somehow been shunted aside by the international community of multilateral organizations.

A number of regional and international bodies play a role in desertification. CILSS was formed in 1973, primarily to co-ordinate the activities and present the views of the eight Sahel countries to potential donors. In the same year, the United Nations established the UN Sudano–Sahelian Office (UNSO) as a response to the Sahel drought. It has special responsibility for all projects in the 19 Sudano–Sahelian countries, and in adjacent areas. A joint venture between UNDP and UNEP in 1978 expanded UNSO's mandate so that it could co-ordinate desertification within the Sudano–Sahelian region. Since then, it has acted on behalf of, and often with financial support from, UNEP.

The Club du Sahel was formed in 1976 by representatives of Western development aid agencies. It has no resources and only a small secretariat (at the Organization for Economic Co-operation and Development in Paris). Yet much of the real communication between donor and recipient nations takes place within the Club. It aims to increase co-operation between Sahel countries and donors, and has the basic objective of achieving food self-sufficiency for Sahel countries.

UNSO and CILSS have been involved in inter-agency rivalry, which has served only to dissipate their energies. They did prepare a joint unified plan for combating desertification in the Sahel, but little has come of it. UNSO, which has its headquarters in New York, has been remarkably ineffective in doing anything about desertification, at least until recently, despite the fact that large amounts of aid are channelled through it. Of a total of $162 million worth of aid for Sahel countries which has come from UNSO, only $13.4 million (8%) had been spent on anti-desertification work by 1980. Much of the UNSO money went on road construction though donors have subsequently admitted that many of these roads could not be justified in terms of agricultural or even economic development. According to UNEP, some $40 million has now been raised by UNSO specifically for anti-desertification projects in the 19 Sudano–Sahelian countries. Certainly, UNSO's anti-desertification record has been improving, though because UNSO is responsible for economic development as well as anti-desertification projects, it is difficult to assess where the money really goes. In a very broad sense, all efforts at economic development in the Sahel could be counted as anti-desertification measures. Intensive agricultural practices, for example, which are adopted by farmers and governments, sometimes stimulated by agencies, in semi-arid areas inevitably require special management because of their particular climatic and soil conditions.

The UN Conference on Desertification (UNCOD) was organized and hosted by the UN Environment Programme (UNEP), and after the conference UNEP set up a Desertification Branch to carry out the tasks assigned to UNEP in UNCOD's Plan of Action (PACD). The Plan also called for the creation of two other bodies: an Inter-Agency Working Group on Desertification (IAWGD), to help co-ordinate activity among UN agencies; and a Consultative Group on Desertification Control (DESCON), comprising representatives of UN agencies, developing countries and funding bodies, to discuss and finance project proposals.

The regional plans requested by the Plan of Action have so far not been prepared. The relevant Economic Commissions

— ECA, ECLA, ECWA and ESCAP — have organized meetings and compiled information, but none has prepared a regional plan or established a research and training centre.[70]

UNEP was given a number of specific responsibilities in co-ordinating anti-desertification action. These were:

(1) to keep a continuous inventory of all desertification projects;

(2) to help prepare the preliminary studies needed to formulate projects;

(3) to prepare alternative proposals for mobilizing the finance needed for anti-desertification projects;

(4) to monitor and evaluate implementation of the Plan of Action on Desertification;

(5) to record the results of desertification monitoring;

(6) to record the results of the monitoring of human populations at risk from desertification;

(7) to publish a newsletter on desertification.

It is interesting to note that none of the above seven 'specific responsibilities' are oriented to corrective action to combat desertification. Rather, they are oriented to a very passive role of monitoring, and recording results of monitoring, or to preparing 'preliminary studies and proposals.'

These responsibilities were supposed to be implemented mainly through the UNEP Desertification Branch together with the management of those desertification-related activities initiated by UNEP before UNCOD.

From its inception in 1973 up to 1984, UNEP approved 25 desertification-related projects to be supported by the UNEP Fund and amounting to a total of $22.6 million, of which UNEP contributed 70.3% or $15.9 million.

Three of these 25 projects were designed for implementation by UNCOD at a total cost of $2.8 million, of which 83% was allocated by the UNEP Fund.

After UNCOD, the UNEP Fund approved 20 desertification projects, allocating $13.2 million, i.e. 68.2% out of a total of $19.4 million.

The creation or reinforcement of this international institutional machinery cost $6.1 million; $2.1 million for the UNEP Desertification Branch and $4 million to strengthen UNSO's anti-desertification activities, leaving only $13.3 million for concrete activities against desertification. Half of this was allocated to five training projects, a figure which underestimates the training activities. Almost all projects include a training component, but for the purpose of this analysis it has not been possible to isolate it. The five projects provided training for 407 technicians at an average cost of $16,216 per trainee. UNEP's contribution to the five training projects amounted to $5.5 million (83%).

Of the remaining funds $5.2 million were for projects having a variety of purposes: to prepare studies, to gather baseline data, to prepare project proposals, to hold seminars and meetings, to prepare a UNEP contribution for the Water Conference, and finally to exchange information (e.g. IPAL projects for Kenya and Tunisia, EMASAR projects for rangelands — both in co-operation with UNESCO — or the green belt projects for North Africa). The preparation of assessment, methodologies and desertification maps (with FAO) as well as a number of information activities and technical assistance matters took the rest.

It appears that the UNEP Desertification Branch has not fulfilled its role of recording the results of the monitoring of desertification and desertification-affected populations. According to a paper prepared for the 12th session of UNEP's Governing Council, the United States 'has benefited very little from UN activities on desertification monitoring. The results of meetings, research, demonstration, etc. have not been synthesized and reported to governments. This is exactly the type of role we believe that the UNEP Desertification Branch should perform.'[71]

UNEP was also charged with keeping a continuous inventory of desertification projects. Co-operation with other United Nations agencies in this matter has proved difficult, although one report was produced.[72] An extraordinary bar chart was included in the general assessment,[73] entitled 'Allocation of actions under recommendations of PACD since 1977, based on an analysis of projects supported by selected agencies and countries'. It purports to show that there have been 801 'actions' (an action is not defined) under 25 different categories. The support organizations listed are 'UNDP, UNEP, UNESCO, Donor Countries, and the World Bank'.

It is not clear why this assessment ignores FAO's contribution to desertification control. In 1984, FAO was supporting land-use planning projects in 16 countries and was running more than 50 projects in soil conservation. FAO claims that 'in Africa alone, 99 FAO projects contributed to the recovery of hundreds of thousands of hectares of agricultural and pasture lands between 1978 and 1982. From 1983, 35 other long-term projects are in progress.'[74]

However, FAO's role in desertification control seems to be often discounted in assessment exercises; no doubt partly because many of its activities pre-date and are not formally connected with the Plan of Action, and also because FAO has a history of poor working relationships with UNEP. This is an unhappy reflection on the state of co-ordination among United Nations agencies.

Another key issue has been the state of knowledge about desertification. Nine years after UNCOD, no one yet knows the exact extent of desertification or the size and location of areas at risk. FAO and UNEP launched a joint desertification assessment and mapping project in 1979, in conjunction with UNESCO, the World Meteorological Organization and the International Society for Soil Science. This produced a 'provisional methodology' which has been tested in nine countries. Work on a world map of desertification hazards was also begun, but appears to have floundered. As FAO points out:[75]

> At present no precise figures are available on areas affected or likely to be affected by desertification; the mapping has been accomplished only on the basis of existing geographic information. There is also no exact data on the rate of the desertification process at global or regional levels, nor in the case of individual countries.

Thus although a lot of discussion has taken place about

the rate of desertification, this has been rather vague, and accurate indicators have not been defined. As Berry noted, 'it is often not possible to determine by how much or even whether conditions have actually deteriorated.'[76]

Thus it seems that one of the priorities for the UNEP Desertification Branch could have been the elaboration of a system of indicators to assess the process. Following the traditional approach in the past, it can be argued that indicators of physical variables and parameters like rainfall, groundwater levels, erosion rate, vegetative cover, etc. do exist. Yet not only has the monitoring of these variables been a difficult task, but it is sometimes misleading and usually insufficient. The fact that such indicators show an isolated physical aspect of change, without taking into account the inter-relationships between them, has been one of their weaknesses.

The second — largely more important — defect has been the complete absence of social variables. Thus although it has been argued that social activities are the main cause of desertification and that concern about desertification arises because human populations are affected, nothing has been done to approach the problem from this angle.

In short, few affected nations have good data on the physical aspects of their own land; fewer still have any data on the socio-economic aspects, which have also been disregarded in desertification assessment activities.

It is therefore scarcely surprising that, when in late 1982 UNEP sent out to 91 affected countries questionnaires on the extent of desertification, from which it expected to gather data to use in its general assessment of progress on the implementation of the Plan, the information gathered was minimal and of virtually no use in the assessment exercise.

The questionnaire was cumbersome, poorly planned and confusing, without a clear conceptual framework and completely unrealistic, reflecting a poor understanding of realities in the affected countries.

Nevertheless a great deal of money and effort was spent on the exercise. In late 1982, UNEP had to mount missions to Lesotho, Botswana, Swaziland, Zambia and Zimbabwe to discuss the questionnaire. Between March and May 1983, further missions were sent to Lesotho, Botswana, Madagascar, Tanzania, Zambia, Zimbabwe, the Economic Commission for Africa's headquarters in Addis Ababa, India, Nepal and Burundi to help governments complete the questionnaire. In addition, 'national experts were identified and recruited in 43 countries to complete the Desertification Questionnaire and prepare country reports.'[77]

In spite of all this, the information that resulted was poor, incomplete and 'not easily comparable'.[78] The experts preparing the final reports had to rely heavily on their personal observations and on what they could glean from discussions with other experts and from the literature.

In relation to the preparation of 'alternative proposals for mobilizing the finance needed for anti-desertification projects', UNEP appointed three expert panels to investigate the situation, and they suggested, among other things, international taxation on trade flows, establishment of a trust fund from gold sales by the IMF, taxes or parking fees on geostationary satellites, levies on revenues from seabed mining and levies on the Common Fund for Commodities. None of these schemes got beyond the stage of proposals, and of course no funds were generated for anti-desertification projects.

Following the recommendation of the Plan of Action on Desertification, two additional institutional mechanisms were created: the Inter-Agency Working Group on Desertification (IAWGD) and the Consultative Group on Desertification Control (DESCON). Both were operated by the UNEP Desertification Branch.

The Inter-Agency Working Group was supposed to bring together the agencies with a role to play in desertification activities in order to:

(1) exchange information on Agency anti-desertification projects;
(2) develop a plan for implementation of the short-term and long-term objectives of the Plan of Action on Desertification;
(3) recommend readjustment of ongoing activities;
(4) formulate projects for co-operative action;
(5) prepare annual reports.

The Consultative Group on Desertification Control (DESCON) is supposed to provide a forum for UN agencies, donor institutions and national governments to identify and mobilize additional resources. In fact, the Consultative Group's activities have been limited to the consideration of project proposals submitted through the Desertification Branch of UNEP.

The Consultative Group screens anti-desertification projects but has had little success in finding finance for them. Indeed, its performance appears to have been deteriorating rapidly. It has held five sessions, of which four were to consider and fund projects. At the second session, 27 projects were considered for which an additional $45.6 million was needed and $17.5 million raised. The third session examined 12 projects for which an additional $20 million was requested and $7.8 million raised. The total additional funds sought to finance the projects submitted at the fourth session amounted to $35.8 million and since then $10.8 million has been raised.[79] So by the end of 1984, the Consultative Group on Desertification Control had sought an additional $103.6 million and obtained $36.1 million. At the last session, nine new projects were submitted and an additional $38.3 million requested.

Developing countries and donors appear to have differing images of the function of the Consultative Group. According to UNEP:

> The latter see the funds available through DESCON as part of the total of bilateral funding; the former regard DESCON as a separate and additional source of funds and tend not to bring forward projects for which direct bilateral funding could be expected. This difference in conception is also reflected in the fact that certain donor countries prefer to be more involved than at present in the process of project design and appear unwilling to enter into formal commitments at the DESCON forum in respect of proposals in the advanced state of formulation in which it is customary to present them.[80]

But these are basic fund-raising problems. All the major UN agencies which work with Trust Funds of one kind or another supplied on a multi– or bilateral basis by donor nations and institutions found ways of coping with them long ago. No explanation has yet been offered why these matters have proved such a problem to the Consultative Group (DESCON).

As Dregne[81] pointed out: 'DESCON has failed to live up to the hope that it would be a new source of funding for anti-desertification projects. Donor agency members have shown a notable lack of enthusiasm to finance projects that have been presented at DESCON meetings, and there is no indication that this situation will change.'

Concerning the Inter-Agency Working Group on Desertification (IAWGD), information has been exchanged but co-ordination remains very poor, while a co-ordinated plan for the achievement of the Plan of Action objectives has not been formulated.

UNEP's Desertification Branch has not been effective in co-ordinating desertification action. The Branch never reached its proposed staffing level, and three years after the UN Conference on Desertification 'this establishment had dwindled down to half the requirement. As a result of financial constraints faced by the whole United Nations system, UNDP and UNFPA could not continue to support the three posts they pledged to finance in 1978.'[82] Although the Branch was meant to be the key desertification unit in the United Nations system, it has become the scapegoat for inaction. This deplorable situation doubtless has explanations at many levels. For example, had the Branch been found to be doing a good job, there seems little doubt that finance for the necessary posts would have been forthcoming — even if not from the original agencies pledged to provide the money, then at least from other sources.

UNEP's job is to catalyse and co-ordinate action. That job is made more difficult by the fact that UNEP has nothing anyone else really wants. On the contrary, most of the other UN agencies involved in desertification tend to resent UNEP's presence, which they regard as an unnecessary complication to their own work. This already difficult relationship has been worsened by UNEP's inability to tread a delicate diplomatic tightrope with anything approaching the neat footwork required.

Other United Nations agencies complain bitterly of UNEP ineptitude and inefficiency, and further inter-agency rivalries have undermined what role it might have been expected to play. As the United States guardedly points out, 'We were concerned that UNEP did not appear to be working as closely as we believed necessary with the CILSS and Club des Amis du Sahel group, and with the UN Sudano–Sahelian Office.'[83] Privately, many delegates from major donor nations went further at the 1984 12th Governing Council of UNEP, which devoted part of its time to reassessing anti-desertification work; they said their governments had not funded projects through UNEP because they did not trust UNEP's ability to use the money efficiently.

Because of chronic under-staffing, the Branch's co-ordination role has amounted to little more than preparing for and attending the IAWGD and DESCON meetings. When UNEP called for a report in 1984 on the institutional and financial impediments to action, its author, Jamaican diplomat E.R. Richardson, was blunt:[84]

> . . . two national plans and nine draft plans constitute the meagre results of five years of effort on the part of (UNEP's) Desertification Branch . . . The Executive Director has not been able at all times to maintain the Desertification Branch at its full strength of eight professionals.

The United States was even more scathing about the role of UN agencies in desertification control. Discussing UNEP's Desertification Branch, IAGWD, DESCON and the Special Account, it claimed that:[85]

> These institutions have, in fact, been largely irrelevant to what has or has not happened in the desertification field since the Plan of Action was approved in 1977. The principal programmes and projects in the field have been designed and implemented by national governments (donors and recipients), institutions such as UNSO, and within the Sahel Development Programme . . . The products and impact of the IAWGD 'co-ordinating' effort are not apparent. The Consultative Group has not been effective in mobilizing additional resources, and the US continues to be concerned that many of the projects it has supported are not of high priority.

The Failures of the Implementing Agencies

Credit must be given to UNEP for one of its activities: it has managed to put desertification on the global agenda of major problems. It has made persistent efforts to alert both governments in affected countries and potential donors to the seriousness of the problem. Global concern has been aroused. That it has not been effectively aroused is the fault partly of the countries affected, partly of the countries who ought to be doing more to help, and partly of the United Nations agencies and bodies which ought to be co-ordinating and implementing action far more effectively.

The latter include a number of the United Nations specialized agencies, notably FAO, UNESCO and the World Meteorological Organization. As already mentioned, UNESCO's arid zone work was established long before UNCOD and, because it was more or less specifically related to desertification, co-ordination of the work within the Plan of Action seems not to have become a major issue. The situation with FAO is quite different.

To the extent that desertification is caused by inappropriate agricultural management and techniques, FAO has a role to play within the UN system in developing the techniques for putting matters right. And indeed FAO is running hundreds of projects which are connected with desertification, some directly and many more indirectly. Yet co-ordination with UNEP appears to have been a major problem. One reason is undoubtedly that action on desertification is the respon-sibility of two of FAO's major technical departments — forestry and agriculture. No division within the Forestry Department is specifically concerned with desertification. Within the Agriculture Department, the Land and Water Division — which implements some 16% of all FAO field projects — includes work on remote sensing, fertilisers, water resources, and soil resources. Again, desertification is not separately featured; indeed, desertification is regarded within FAO simply as one issue among many in the general areas of soil erosion and conservation, water management, and reforestation and afforestation.

Although FAO's contribution to desertification control is one of the most important within the UN system, FAO itself has made little effort to co-ordinate its own work on desertification, or to work effectively in conjunction with UNEP. While FAO feels it has been underused in implementing the Plan of Action, it has done little to help things along except for creating a small Environment Programme Co-ordinating Unit. If desertification is to be effectively controlled, the FAO's major contribution will have to be far more effectively co-ordinated with action elsewhere in the United Nations system.

6. Some Successes

An exceedingly gloomy picture has been painted of anti-desertification work. Neither affected poor countries, nor wealthy aid-giving countries, nor international agencies seem willing to make the efforts required to keep threatened areas productive.

It is regrettable that large amounts of money failed to have a significant effect. It may be argued that initiatives take time to develop and produce results, that money is not necessarily wasted even if the problem has not been solved in the short term. However, it is questionable how much of those resources and efforts were specifically devoted to dealing with the causes of desertification. A substantial amount of aid is used simply on food aid, information, meetings and training. This picture might give the impression that desertification is an insoluble problem. This is not true. Development does offer mechanisms for coping with desertification.

During the late 18th and early 19th centuries in the United States, Great Plains farmers tended to overcultivate, deforest and allow their stock to overgraze. But these farmers gained political power as their territories became states. Federal and state crop insurance programmes, soil conservation services, land-use laws, forestry services, feed and grain reserves, rural credit and electrification schemes and rural education schemes were instituted. Universities and other organizations and institutions offered drought and disease-resistant crop varieties and new techniques for conserving soil and water. Desertification remains a problem in the United States, and the West, Mid-West and South still suffer occasional droughts; but the coping mechanisms are in place and working. Australia has achieved similar progress.

During its own period of agricultural and industrial development, the United States had considerable advantages over most dryland Third World countries today (abundant, valuable natural resources; investment capital; slow population growth and room for expansion, among others). Dryland Third World countries are hardly in a position to copy such coping mechanisms. But the success of many anti-desertification projects shows that the technical means are there.

There are many isolated cases of impressive anti-desertification projects. In Bouza in Southern Niger, every street is lined with trees, and the town is being encircled by woods. Green belts are being planted around the capital cities of Ouagadougou and Niamey in Burkina Faso and Niger. An irrigation project in Tunisia has increased agricultural production 27-fold. Algeria has planted 267,500 hectares of forests. Ethiopian peasant associations have terraced the heavily eroded land on some 35 watersheds of the central highland plateau, and planted trees for fuelwood and fruit on them. Some 1,500 km of roadside shelter belts are being planted in the State of Rajasthan in India. Sudan is restocking its gum belt, which acts as a barrier to the desert. Peru has begun an $80 million programme to reforest its Andean Sierra. Some 10,000 hectares of sand dunes are being stabilized annually in Rajasthan.

China has largely proved that the creation of a large green belt is a feasible target. A shelterbelt 1,500 km long and 12 metres wide was established by some 700,000 farmers. China has built three green belts, one of 1,200 km in Mongolia. In the last 30 years, China has developed a programme of mass afforestation at a rate of 1.5 million hectares per year.

China has also reclaimed large desertified areas: for example, using casuarina trees for coastal windbreaks 57 km long and 1 to 5 km wide on Nanshan Island in Guangdong Province. The yields in recovered areas have since trebled.

In Chifeng, using 'mass mobilization', 20,000 hectares of sand dunes of about 0.1 to 0.5 hectares each were levelled, flooded with silty water and transformed. Later paddy fields were established together with protective shelterbelts against sand encroachment.

The reclamation of desertified areas in the Kara Kum is an important example of a very large project. The Kara Kum Desert stretches for more than 500 miles across southern Soviet Central Asia, covering a large part of Turkmenistan. The desert has been crossed by a 870 mile long canal which drains the Amu Darya River into the Caspian Sea. The canal, which is navigable for half of its length, increased available irrigated land from 300,000 to 650,000 hectares and cotton production rose from 100,000 tonnes to over a million tonnes. In addition and with the main purpose of controlling water weeds, herbivorous fish have been introduced, providing an important source of animal protein for the local population.[86]

It should be emphasized that many of the activities of the small, non-governmental organizations (NGOs) have also proved successful, largely because they usually depend critically on the involvement of local people. For example, the US voluntary agency CARE has helped establish 250 km of windbreaks in Niger's Majia valley, whereas many larger afforestation schemes in the Sahel have come seriously unstuck. Project officers proved to the people the ability of those windbreaks to increase crop yields; and developed with the people a process of sharing out the income from the sale of pruned wood. Anti-desertification techniques introduced into Burkina Faso by the British-based voluntary agency, Oxfam, are being spread from village to village by the farmers themselves, because they work and make use of village resources.

Dozens of NGOs around the world have become involved, 'above all, in field projects such as tree planting and soil and water conservation, but also in schemes to supplement food production in subsistence communities as well as in training and in increasing environmental awareness at the local level. Their success is related to the small scale and local direction of their projects and the requirements for local community participation, as well as their flexibility in operation and their ability to learn from earlier mistakes. The dominance of field activities gives these actions an impact out of proportion to the money invested.'[87] Yet, while the activity of NGOs can demonstrate possibilities, the scale of both their financial and human resources — and thus the scale of their activities — will always be far too small to make a dent in the massive problem of desertification. It is doubtless right for governments and UN agencies to encourage them, but it would be a mistake to rely upon them.

Many other projects could be added to this list, showing what can technically be achieved. All of these worthy efforts, however, may be overwhelmed by the present drought in the Sahel, just as many of the five million seedlings planted over the past seven years by Ethiopian peasant associations have been killed by the present drought. Nevertheless, it is worth concentrating on a few major projects in rangeland management, food production and security, and reforestation. In each area, the project or projects described are major efforts which hold considerable promise for the future.

Rangeland Management

Although attempts at rangeland management, and improving conditions for nomadic pastoralists, have been perhaps the least successful of all anti-desertification efforts, a programme in Syria has demonstrated that the problem can be tackled. It has broad and important implications for rangeland management exercises elsewhere, particularly in the Sahel.

In Syria, sheep production is the major livestock activity, based on the steppe grazing area which covers 121 million hectares, 58% of the country. A three-year drought during 1958–60 reduced the sheep population from 5.9 to 2.9 million. The government then began a steppe improvement programme. A special Steppe Department was set up and efforts made to improve conditions for the bedouins and their flocks. By 1980, the sheep population had climbed to 8.8 million.

Grazing co-operatives were established to limit over-grazing and destruction of the ranges. Each co-operative was given the sole right to graze certain demarcated areas and each family in the co-operative granted a licence to graze a specified number of sheep (100–125). Efforts were made to keep the sheep off the ranges during critical times of the year. In effect, the new system was a revival of the ancient *hema* system of range management formerly practised by the bedouins. By 1981, there were 105 co-operatives grazing 2.5 million sheep on 6 million hectares of rangeland.

Initially, the bedouins were afraid of losing their independence, and their co-operation was difficult to obtain. But the programme started slowly, only expanding as the pastoralists gained confidence in it. Fattening units were set up on a co-operative basis in cereal-producing areas to limit the dependence of the bedouins on traders and to reduce pressure on grazing land. By 1981, there were 55 of these co-operatives, with 4,400 members, fattening 1.5 million sheep. Research provided them with efficient fattening rations.

As in the Sahel, the spread of cultivation to low rainfall areas of the rangelands had caused large areas to degenerate. Laws were passed which prohibited ploughing and cultivation of rangelands within the steppe. Some 7,000 hectares were planted with drought resistant shrubs. In the wetter areas, production of forage crops during fallow periods provided additional dry season feed for the sheep. Between 1974 and 1979, the area under forage crops and pulses increased nearly tenfold, from 8,600 hectares to 83,700 hectares. To improve water availability, a number of surface dams and deep wells were constructed. Some 2,800 ruined Roman water cisterns were restored in the last four years of the programme.

The Syrian experience shows that it is possible to improve rangelands, to get fiercely independent pastoralists to co-operate, and to integrate them into a modern economic system without destroying their lifestyles.

Food Crops and Food Security

Of the Sahel countries, only Niger could claim food self-sufficiency in early 1984 and only Niger was not on the FAO list of African countries threatened with starvation. The reasons are not geographical. With 5.7 million people, an average GNP per capita of $330 a year and life expectancy of only 45 years,[88] Niger is one of the least developed countries in the world. Yet the country is self-sufficient in its two staple foods, sorghum and millet, if the harvest is good. In a wet year production can reach 1.25 million tonnes. Unlike Mali and Senegal, Niger does not benefit from long stretches of rivers. Furthermore, Niger did not inherit irrigation systems from colonial times, and no major dam has been built since independence in 1960.[89]

However, it must be considered that Niger has been able to capitalize on the exports of one important natural resource — uranium. During the 1970s this was the main reason for an astonishing growth in the country's merchandise exports, which grew by an average of 23.4% per annum over an 11-year period, compared to 7.1% for Mali and −1.4% for Senegal.[90] Niger has used much of its additional income in a direct assault on rural poverty.

Since 1974, President Seyni Kountché has insisted on giving agriculture priority in development goals. Peasant taxes have been reduced and much of the state budget has been spent on building up rural infrastructure, providing a health system for the rural population and extension services for farmers. Even more important, by buying stocks of cereals at reasonable prices, the government has controlled and stabilized the price of grain and provided incentives for farmers to produce more. Reserve grain stocks have also been built up for use in times of emergency.

Furthermore, international aid has been used to good effect to support these policies. After the Sahel drought, Niger decided to establish a grain reserve of 40,000 tonnes — enough to feed the most vulnerable half of the population for a month and a half in the event of further drought. West Germany provided $3.3 million to buy 18,000 tonnes of grain, but another drought struck and the food was sold or distributed to the needy almost immediately.

Another West German grant, plus contributions arranged through FAO, enabled Niger to buy more cereals, build warehouses to store it, and purchase some of the equipment needed to set up a reserve cereal stock. Even so, not all the country's needs could be met. The Dutch government then funded a project for storing another 6,500 tonnes of grain, treating the grain against pests and providing a laboratory for quality control and research on storage losses. Thirteen more warehouses were built, each holding 500 tonnes of grain in sacks, and sited at strategic places throughout the country. The project was complemented by World Food Programme funds for the purchase of 18,000 tonnes of grain, and an Arab Bank for Economic Development in Africa grant to provide storage for another 5,000 tonnes of grain.

Niger decided later to increase its grain reserves, first to 115,000 tonnes and later to 140,000 tonnes. Some of the additional storage is to increase the size of the emergency reserve to 65,000 tonnes, but the function of most is to help stabilize agricultural prices. A further ten warehouses were built. The strategic reserve is operated by the *Organisation de la Production Vivrière du Niger* (OPVN), which buys up the millet surplus immediately after harvest, thus guaranteeing that prices cannot be manipulated by traders.

Niger's system of advice and extension for farmers is probably the best in the Sahel. There is less emphasis on cash crops — undoubtedly because of the alternative export potential of uranium ore — and the government sets a good example to the rest of the country. In 1983, for example, 5,000 cattle were sold from government farms as a warning to pastoralists that grazing would be insufficient for several months to come. The government advised herders to move to better pastures and began to lay on animal fodder to help get the herds through the 1983–84 dry season.[91] Niger's efforts show both the way forward and the willingness of the government to embark on this path.

Reforestation

Reforestation is one of the keys to desertification control. In

107

the Sahel, it has met with limited success. Even where trees have been successfully introduced in Sahel countries — as in several village woodlot schemes in Senegal, for example — the projects have often been designed primarily to alleviate fuelwood and building pole shortages rather than control desertification. However, one of the attractions of village tree-planting schemes is that they can provide simultaneous solutions to many different problems. Trees provide fuelwood, poles, fruit, nuts, and animal fodder, increase rural incomes, improve soil fertility, help control erosion and take the pressure off natural trees and forests. An important aspect in reforestation is the rights of ownership (collective or individual) over both the land and the trees.

South Korea has been the major success story of village forestry. In the early 1960s, fuelwood supplies there became critically short, and tree felling on steep slopes led to severe soil erosion and flooding. Each village was therefore encouraged by the government to set up a Village Forestry Association (VFA), which received a subsidy and was awarded land on which trees could be planted or on which degraded forest could be restored. Within five years, 20,000 VFAs were in existence, more than one million hectares had been planted (about one–quarter for fuelwood, the rest for fruit and timber), 4.4 million hectares of degraded forest had been brought under management and more than 3 billion seedlings planted. What had originally been conceived as a ten-year programme was effectively achieved in six years.

The success of this project was due to a number of factors, which have since been carefully analysed for their relevance to community forestry as a whole.[92] One of the keys was that the government was able and prepared to pass legislation which granted the VFAs title to the land they managed. Another was that the villagers involved were already committed to the idea of rural development, and had had some experience of co-operative forestry schemes before.

But the way the project was implemented was also important. Mechanisms were introduced which enabled the VFAs and government to co-operate effectively, in a manner which combined 'top-down' and 'bottom-up' planning. The VFAs were also provided with the materials, finance and information they needed quickly and efficiently, and they were not asked to do too much too quickly; a step-by-step approach was adopted. Careful research also established exactly which species were likely to be most effective, and some 'quick return' tree crops were included in all schemes to give villagers early remuneration for their efforts. Every hectare planted with fuelwood trees was matched by half a hectare planted with chestnuts, and the production of mushrooms, fibre, bark, resins and other non-wood products encouraged. By 1978, these products were generating an income of $100 million a year for the more than two million families involved in the programme.

Currently, the most successful community forestry project is taking place in Nepal, where much hill land has been severely deforested. Here again, government action has enabled small local administrative groups, called *panchayats*, to take over replanted land. To help the *panchayats* plan and execute their work, the government also set up a Community and Afforestation Division within its Forestry Department.

The 340 *panchayats* involved in the project are establishing nurseries to provide 900,000 seedlings, replanting 11,750 hectares with seedlings and protecting 39,100 hectares of damaged forest. In addition, 15,000 improved wood stoves are being introduced, enough to save 25,000 tons of fuelwood a year.

The five-year project is being supported by FAO, UNDP and the World Bank at a total cost of $24.8 million. Eventually, the project should provide about one–third of the fuelwood requirements of 570,000 people and enough leaf fodder for 132,000 cattle. It is estimated that, because less dung and crop waste will be used as fuel, as much as 156,000 tons of grain a year will be saved, nearly one–third of the total production of the hill region.

7. Conclusions

The battle against desertification and the recovery of desertified areas is by definition a long–term process. However, the adoption of a long–term perspective in fighting desertification is hindered by the pressures of the immediate humanitarian aspects. Action is needed now to alleviate the plight of large populations affected by desertification.

On the other hand, if these people are not helped, they will exert more pressure over a weak natural system, thus accelerating desertification. Immediate action in favour of the large affected communities is not therefore a simple humanitarian action, but it also has a strategic role in the battle against desertification. Desertification gives rise to new forces that tend to reinforce the process: it creates poverty and poverty in turn pushes people to adopt measures that reinforce the desertification process.

Therefore, desertification requires strategies which explicitly include short-term and long-term actions, palliative measures as well as actions against the structural causes of the phenomenon.

Desertification is the result of increasing interactions between different economic activities of dryland societies and the cyclical fluctuations of nature. Social causes of desertification have been intensified in the last decades because of the changing economic patterns of dryland societies and their increasing integration into the international system. This means that local solutions alone, distinct from international dynamics, will not be able to cope with the problem.

The different socio-economic causes of desertification are interrelated. The clear identification and assessment of all their interrelationships is therefore a prerequisite to any effective action. What is needed is simultaneous action to stop deforestation and to accelerate afforestation, to avoid overgrazing and to recover arid lands, to reduce monoculture activities and to provide alternatives to local harmful activities in pursuit of basic food, fuelwood, water, health and shelter needs.

Desertification is at the heart of the development problematic of many countries and, in fact, of large regions of the world. The process is jeopardizing the complete process of development but, at the same time, lack of development is preventing any action against desertification. And action can only be successful if it is an integral part of a comprehensive development plan and strategy.

In this context it is wrong to believe that rural development — or the lack of it — is the only key to the desertification process. Practices harmful to the natural resources of arid and semi-arid areas also stem from the lack of development of urban areas. It should not be forgotten that 20% to 30% of dryland populations live in urban areas which exert additional pressure on the immediate hinterlands, through their increasing demand for fuelwood, water, etc.

In addition, food pricing policies which tend to subsidize city dwellers at the expense of those living in the countryside, and favour the production of specific crops better suited to city tastes, also have a negative effect, though less directly so. Thus the urban–rural division within the country reproduces the international phenomenon of unfavourable terms of trade. Therefore, desertification should be viewed as an explicit dimension not just of rural development, but of development as a whole.

Desertification issues should be included not only in the normative part of development plans but also in the elaboration of strategies and at the operative level of planning. This requires the development of appropriate and sound management practices for arid and semi-arid areas. Land should be used in accordance with the potential and constraints of the soil, avoiding the transfer and use of inadequate technology introduced for the sake of short-term commercial returns.

To integrate desertification in national development planning, the main actors and their roles in the process must be clearly identified as well as the mechanisms needed for them to achieve maximum efficiency. These actors are in fact social groups.

The actors to be considered are the governments and policy-implementing institutions in arid and semi-arid zones, the private cash-crop or ranching landlords or companies, the peasants and the pastoral population of arid and semi-arid areas, international agencies active in these areas, the international community as a whole (because of the pressure they create on arid and semi-arid lands through their demands for specific commodities), and finally scientific and technological professionals dealing with the problem of desertification.

Among the actors women deserve special consideration because of their predominant role in the production of food crops (more than 90% in the case of Africa), in the collection of fuelwood and cowdung, which increases deforestation and decreases soil fertility, in fetching water and in taking care of goats and sheep. This role is also increasing in Africa, with the move of young men to urban areas because of desertification.

But it is not enough to identify the main actors dealing with desertification if adequate technical and economic resources are not provided. To the extent that soil erosion and desertification are among the major disasters of some developing countries, they must be explicitly considered in development planning. Disaster prevention must be part of development planning. Early warning systems based on physical and meteorological data should be combined with social indicators so as to respond not only to weather signals but also to market and social distress signals.

Institutional mechanisms also should be identified and created to allow the different actors to co-ordinate their efforts. This is especially relevant in the case of desertification, as it implies that global policies of a national and even international character must be co-ordinated and implemented through decentralized mechanisms at the local level. Indeed, while desertification is a global process, it varies from place to place according to national characteristics — types of soil and the habits and patterns of development of the local people.

By taking the local dimension into account it is possible to make use of the local potentialities and avoid the adoption and application of actions unsuited to local, natural and socio-economic conditions. Inevitably, therefore, an essential element will be participation, i.e. involvement of all the actors dealing with the problem or affected by it to define policies and strategies at all levels and design, implement and control programmes for the development of arid and semi-arid regions.

But there again, mechanisms are useless without adequate financial and technical resources. In both cases international action has an extremely important role to play. Most of the drylands of the world and almost all the people affected by desertification are in developing countries. These countries are facing extremely difficult economic situations because of their debt burden and deteriorating terms of trade. They lack the financial resources necessary to alleviate the plight of those most immediately affected, while strategic reserves of food that can be used for aid are non-existent. Food aid therefore has to be an international concern.

But it is extremely important to provide the right kind of aid at the right time and in such a way as not to have negative socio-economic effects. A clear understanding of the socio-cultural features of aid recipients is therefore indispensable.

The fight against the causes of desertification and for the recovery of deteriorated areas is a long-term process which requires a regular flow of resources — to implement measures that will yield results only in the long term and to provide short-term assistance to preserve the effectiveness of long-term measures. Once a programme to combat desertification is initiated in one area, it must not be interrupted.

International co-operation between affected countries,

national governments and international institutions, together with technical assistance, is required for this long-term aspect of the anti-desertification action. However, it should be clear that this international, more centralized policy will be effective only if it is based on the local capabilities and understanding of the problem.

Global policies and strategies of a centralized character must be consistent with their decentralized implementation, at the local level.

Scientific and technological resources have a strategic role to play in the development of arid and semi-arid regions, in arresting the desertification process and in recovering areas already desertified. There are many aspects of the science and technology issue relating to desertification. One is the penetration of technologies mainly to increase the productivity of cash crop areas, and their impact on natural systems. A second is the retreat of traditional technology developed by societies living in these areas and suited to their constraints and potentialities. A third is the relative backwardness generally of science and technology for the management of arid and semi-arid lands.

The first technological issue is the result of the modernization of croplands in order to achieve a level of productivity for integration into international markets. Historically, modernization is carried out by the simple transfer of technologies used in temperate zones where conditions and soils are different. When transferred, there is, indeed, a short-term increase in productivity, but in the long run the soil deteriorates because of heavy machinery, deep ploughing and reduction of biological diversity, thus increasing the vulnerability of the system to natural and social hazards.

However, the few years of increasing productivity allowed those farmers with access to modern technology to increase their economic power and gain control over larger cropping areas and water resources in order to compensate for declining productivity. In effect, therefore, technological penetration means less land available for grazing, fewer nomadic routes, more pressure on the land, overgrazing, and ultimately desertification.

From a purely technological point of view, imported technology goes against traditional indigenous technologies which are regarded as obsolescent. The logical approach concerning technology requires careful screening of foreign technology, an assessment of ecological feasibility in arid and semi-arid regions, and an effort to blend them with indigenous technology. Simultaneously, indigenous technology should be upgraded by the application of scientific and technological knowledge.

Unfortunately, because of desertification, traditional local technology is no longer adequate in many cases, for example, because of the reduction of pastures or because of the loss of some genetic varieties.

The third scientific and technological issue refers to the almost total lack of technology development for the management and recovery of arid and semi-arid lands. Research is urgently needed into the characteristics of these arid and semi-arid areas in order to develop suitable technologies. This includes studies of the most appropriate farming systems for each region including agroforestry, animal husbandry, etc; the study and development of appropriate irrigation schemes; research into genetic varieties of arid and semi-arid areas and their potentialities as generators of important economic activities and in general the development of biotechnologies for the use of available biological resources; and research into combining modern and indigenous technologies and upgrading indigenous technologies by applying modern scientific methods. The use of new, high-yield sorghum varieties already tested in India and Sudan should be promoted throughout arid and semi-arid areas.

The management of arid and semi-arid areas should also be studied to plan soil use adapted to biological productivity, the potential of their diversity and their seasonality. For example, the cash crop/food crop ratio should be assessed for each area as well as the type of husbandry most suitable for them.

This planning should consider a pricing policy rather more complex than the one usually applied. This pricing policy should be combined with financial assistance.

Clearly, low returns in arid and semi-arid lands are partly to blame for the lack of investment. But so is the dynamic of a cyclical drought–famine process which makes debtors unable to repay their loans or get new loans after the drought when they need them most urgently. Furthermore it is important to revise the traditional credit schemes which allocate resources to farmers as individual operators when the fight against desertification requires collective action.

The approach suggested considers that desertification can only be halted and avoided in the context of the overall process of development.

The humanitarian issues associated with desertification are inherent in the lack of development of the areas affected. Ultimately, the only real weapon against desertification is sustainable development.

The lack of development is indeed a humanitarian issue in itself. Desertification jeopardizes the process of development, creating at the same time an immediate human drama.

'Desertification' and not 'desertization' was the concept adopted by UNCOD because, while the latter put the emphasis on the material causes and dimension of the phenomenon, the former holds social activity as primarily responsible for it. Yet the review of activities since UNCOD shows a concentration of studies and projects on the physical aspects of the problem, neglecting the human dimension.

However, the physical disruption is associated with a dramatic deterioration of the social conditions of dryland people, leading to a process of disintegration of their traditional social fabric. Both physical and social deterioration broke down old mechanisms without replacing them by new ones.

Social disintegration reinforces the physical process of desertification, which, in turn, increases the vulnerability of dryland people and destroys their social and economic security.

Dryland people are quite aware of the phenomenon, yet, due to the combination of economic, social and natural forces, they are compelled, in their fight for survival, to continue to exploit ever more marginal land for ever smaller yields. The scale of deterioration means that the local

117

population can no longer cope.

The social dimension behind desertification is a complex one; it combines particular conditions, behaviours, values and beliefs and institutional arrangements. The concrete manifestations of dryland conditions are an unequal distribution of resources, poverty, poor health and nutritional status, illiteracy, low expectancy of life at birth, and infant mortality. These conditions interact with behaviours concerning size of family, roles of social members, size of livestock flocks and herds and with values and beliefs like those concerning fertility, the sanctity of cows or their slaughter and castration, or beliefs that may prevent the penetration of alternative solutions.

The combination of such factors, associated with prevailing economic structures and policies like land tenure and credit policies, tend to make things worse.

Finally, the incorporation of dryland societies into the world system means new difficulties because of the need to compete in world markets and because of new consumption patterns.

All these elements have often been ignored in the fight against desertification. As the African writer Aye Kwe-Armah put it: 'It is a wonder we have been flung so far from the way.'

References

1. Relief and Rehabilitation Commission (Ethiopia), 1975. *Drought Rehabilitation in Wollo and Tigre.* Addis Ababa, RRC.
2. UNEP, 1983. UNEP Desertification Branch. *Activities Related to Combating Desertification and Drought.* UNEP/WG.102/3.
3. Zachariah K.C. and Condé Julien, 1981. *Migration in West Africa: Demographic Aspects*, World Bank, Oxford University Press, Oxford.
4. Eckholm, Erik, 1984. 'Poverty, Population Growth and Desertification' in *Desertification Control,* No. 10.
5. FAO, 1981. 'Tree planting for energy and development of rural communities in the Sierra', Rome, FAO, Plan of Operation GCP/PER027/NET.
6. UNEP, 1984. *General Assessment of Progress in the Implementation of the Plan of Action to Combat Desertification.* Report of the Executive Director. Nairobi, UNEP, UNEP/GC.12/9.
7. World Bank, 1984. *Toward Sustained Development in Sub-Saharan Africa: A Joint Program of Action.* Washington, D.C., World Bank.
8. FAO, 1983. 'Production problems in Sub-Saharan Africa' in *World Food Report 1983.* Rome, FAO.
9. Twose, Nigel, 1984. *Behind the Weather: Why the Poor Suffer Most: Drought and the Sahel.* Oxford, Oxfam Public Affairs Unit.
10. UNEP, 1984. *General Assessment . . . ,* op. cit.
11. Richardson, E.R., 1983. *Evaluation of International and Financial Arrangements.* Nairobi, UNEP.

119

12. UNEP, 1984. *General Assessment* . . . , op. cit.
13. Richardson, E.R., 1983. Op. cit.
14. Dregne, Harold E., 1984. 'Combating Desertification: Evaluation of Progress' in *Environmental Conservation*, Vol. 11, Nos. 1 & 2 (Spring and Summer Issues).
15. Dregne, Harold E., 1984. Op. cit.
16. UNEP, 1984. *General Assessment* . . . , op. cit.
17. Mabutt, J.A., 1983. *Assessment of the Status and Trend of Desertification.* Nairobi, UNEP.
18. United States, 1984. *Views and Recommendations on Progress made in Implementing the Plan of Action to Combat Desertification.* Nairobi, paper prepared for 12th Session of UNEP Governing Council.
19. Dregne, H.E., 1983. *Evaluation of the Implementation of the Plan of Action to Combat Desertification.* Nairobi, UNEP.
20. Berry, L., 1984. 'Desertification in the Sudano–Sahelian Region 1977–1984' in *Desertification Control*, No. 10.
21. Tolba, M.K, 1984. 'Harvest of dust' in *Desertification Control Bulletin*, No. 10.
22. Club du Sahel/CILSS, 1980. *The Sahel Drought Control and Development Programme, 1975–79: A Review and Analysis.* Paris, Club du Sahel.
23. Economic Commission for Africa (ECA), 1980. *Plan of Action for the Implementation of the Monrovia Strategy for the Economic Development of Africa.* (Lagos Plan of Action) E/CN 14/781/Add. 1 April 1980.
24. UNEP, 1984. *General Assessment* . . . , op. cit.
25. Dregne, H.E., 1983. *Evaluation of the Implementation*, op. cit.
26. FAO, 1983. *Preliminary Report on Public Expenditure on Agriculture in Developing Countries.* Rome, FAO.
27. FAO, 1984. *How Development Strategies Benefit the Rural Poor*. Rome, FAO.
28. FAO, 1984. 'The attack on rural poverty' in *World Food Report 1984.* Rome, FAO.
29. FAO, 1984. *How Development Strategies* . . . , op. cit.
30. United States, 1984. Op. cit.
31. FAO, 1984. *How Development Strategies* . . . , op. cit.
32. Ibid.
33. Ibid.
34. Olive, M. McGraw, 1984. 'Major Determinants of Agricultural Production Decreases, 1975–83, in Sub-Saharan Africa.' Personal communication.
35. Olive, M. McGraw. 1984. Op. cit.

36. Twose, Nigel, 1984. Op. cit.
37. FAO, 1983. *Production Problems* . . . , op. cit.
38. FAO, 1984. 'Stocks, ability and access' in *World Food Report 1984*. Rome, 1984.
39. Twose, Nigel, 1984. Op. cit.
40. Clarke, Robin, (in press). *FAO and Agfund*. Rome, FAO, 1985.
41. FAO, 1983. *Production Problems* . . . , op. cit.
42. FAO, 1983. *Preliminary Report* . . . , op. cit.
43. World Bank, 1983. *World Development Report 1983*. New York and Oxford, Oxford University Press.
44. Jackson, Tony, 1982. *Against the Grain*. Oxford, Oxfam.
45. Meuer, Gerd, 1984. 'How to hit the hunger list'. Cologne, mimeo.
46. FAO, 1984. *External Assistance to Agriculture: Changing Patterns and Dimensions*. Rome, FAO.
47. FAO, 1984. *World Food, Hunger and Commodity Trade Problems*. Paper prepared for the Council of Europe Conference 'North–South: Europe's role', Lisbon, 9–11 April 1984. Rome, FAO.
48. FAO, 1984. *External Assistance* . . . , op. cit.
49. FAO, 1983. *Review of Field Programmes 1982–83*. Rome, FAO.
50. FAO, 1984. *External assistance* . . . , op. cit.
51. FAO, 1979. *Report of the World Conference on Agrarian Reform and Rural Development*. FAO, Rome.
52. Grainger, Alan, 1982. *Desertification: How People Make Deserts, How People Can Stop and Why They Don't*. London, Earthscan.
53. Eckholm, E., Foley, G., Barnard, G., and Timberlake, L., 1984. *Fuelwood: The Energy Crisis That Won't Go Away*. London, Earthscan.
54. Quinti, Gabriele, 1984. 'Cinque Anni di Interventi Nei Paesi Del Sahel' in *Cooperazione* No. 39.
55. FAO, 1984. *How Development Strategies* . . . , op. cit.
56. FAO, 1984. *External Assistance* . . . , op. cit.
57. Clark, Robin, 1983. 'An insurance against drought' in *Cooperation through Trust*. Rome, FAO.
58. FAO, 1984. *External Assistance* . . . , op. cit.
59. FAO, 1983. *Production Problems* . . . , op. cit.
60. FAO, 1983. *The State of Food and Agriculture 1982*. Rome, FAO.
61. FAO, 1984. *World Food, Hunger* . . . , op. cit.

62. Club du Sahel/CILSS, 1980. *The Sahel Drought* . . . , op. cit.
63. The World Bank, 1984. *Towards Sustained Development* . . . , op. cit.
64. FAO, 1984. *A Guide to Staple Foods of the World.* Rome, FAO.
65. Swaminathan M.S., 1985. 'Africa may one day feed us all' in *Development Forum*, April 1985.
66. FAO, 1983. *Production Problems* . . . , op. cit.
67. Berry L. 1983. 'Assessment of Desertification in the Sudano–Sahelian Region' (*Multi-disciplinary Meeting on the Impact of Drought on Socio-Economic Systems in Africa*) December 1983.
68. World Bank, 1984. *Toward Sustained Development*, op. cit.
69. Ibid.
70. UNEP, 1984. *Activities of the United Nations Environment Programme in the Combat against Desertification.* Nairobi, UNEP.
71. United States, 1984. *Views & Recommendations* . . . , op. cit.
72. UNEP, 1982. *Compendium of Projects and Programmes of the United Nations System in the Field of Desertification.* Nairobi, UNEP.
73. UNEP, 1984. *General Assessment* . . . , op. cit.
74. FAO (in press). *FAO's Activities in Combating Desertification.* Rome, FAO.
75. Ibid.
76. Berry L. 1984. *Desertification*, op. cit.
77. UNEP, 1984. *Activities of the UNEP* . . . , op. cit.
78. Berry L. 1984. *Desertification* . . . , op. cit.
79. UNEP, 1984. *Activities of the UNEP* . . . , op. cit.
80. UNEP, 1984. *General Assessment* . . . . op. cit.
81. Dregne, H.E. 1984. *Combating Desertification* . . . , op. cit.
82. UNEP, 1984. *General Assessment* . . . , op. cit.
83. United States 1984. *Views and Recommendations* . . . , op. cit.
84. Richardson., E.R. 1983. Op. cit.
85. United States, 1984. *Views and Recommendations* . . . , op. cit.
86. Voskresenki, 1977. 'Making The Desert Bloom' in *World Health*, July 1977.
87. UNEP, 1984. *General Assessment* . . . , op. cit.
88. World Bank, 1983. *World Development Report* . . . , op. cit.
89. Meuer, Gerd, 1984. Op. cit.
90. World Bank, 1983. *World Development Report* . . . , op. cit.
91. Earthscan, 1984. *Natural Disasters: Acts of God – Or Acts of Man.* London, Earthscan, Earthscan Press Briefing Document No. 39.

92. Gregerson, H.M., 1982. *Village Forestry Development in the Republic of Korea – A Case Study.* Rome, FAO, Forestry for Local Community Development Series.
93. Farouk El Baz and Ted A. Maxwell (Editors), 1982. *Desert Landforms of Southwest Egypt: A Basis for Comparison with Mars.* Washington, D.C., NASA CR-3611.

Appendix: Information Note on the Independent Commission on International Humanitarian Issues

The establishment of an Independent Commission on International Humanitarian Issues is the response of a group of eminent persons from all parts of the world to the deeply felt need to enhance public awareness of important humanitarian issues and to promote an international climate favouring progress in the humanitarian field.

The work of the Commission is intended to be a part of the continuing search of the world community for a more adequate international framework to uphold human dignity and rise to the challenge of colossal humanitarian problems arising with increasing frequency in all continents.

In 1981, the UN General Assembly adopted by consensus a resolution relating to a 'new international humanitarian order' in which it recognized: 'the importance of further improving a comprehensive international framework which takes fully into account existing instruments relating to humanitarian questions as well as the need for addressing those aspects which are not yet adequately covered'. In doing so, the Assembly bore in mind that 'institutional arrangements and actions of governmental and non-governmental bodies might need to be further strengthened to respond effectively in situations requiring humanitarian action.'

The following year, the General Assembly adopted by consensus a further resolution relating to the International Humanitarian Order noting 'the proposal for establishment, outside the United Nations framework, of an "Independent Commission on International Humanitarian Issues" composed of leading personalities in the humanitarian field or having wide experience of government or world affairs.'

The Independent Commission on International Humanitarian Issues was inaugurated in July 1983 and held its first plenary meeting in New York in November 1983. A few days later, the UN General Assembly adopted another resolution in which it noted the establishment of the Commission and requested the Secretary-General to remain in contact with governments as well as with the Independent Commission in order to provide a comprehensive report on the humanitarian order to the Assembly.

In 1985, the United Nations Secretary-General presented to the General Assembly a comprehensive report and comments from governments on the 'new international humanitarian order'. The report included a description of the Independent Commission and its work. In a subsequent resolution adopted by consensus, the General Assembly took note of the activities of the Commission and looked forward to the outcome of its efforts and its Final Report.

Composition of the Commission

The Commission is an independent body whose members participate in their personal capacity and not as representatives of governments or international bodies to which they may belong. Its work is not intended to interfere with governmental negotiations or inter-state relations nor to duplicate work being done by existing governmental or non-governmental bodies.

In its deliberations, the Commission benefits from the advice of governments, existing international governmental and non-governmental bodies and leading experts. The Commission operates through a small Secretariat which coordinates research activities and provides support services for the work of the Commission. The composition of the Commission, which is intended to remain limited, is based on equitable geographical distribution. At present, it has twenty-seven members.

Programme of Work

In the course of its limited life span of three years, 1983–1986, the Commission has dealt with a wide range of subjects relating to humanitarian issues of relevance to contemporary society. The main areas which have been selected by the Independent Commission for study are:

(i)   Humanitarian norms in the context of armed conflicts.

(ii)   Natural and man-made disasters.

(iii)   Vulnerable groups requiring special care and protection such as refugees and displaced persons, stateless persons, children and youth, indigenous populations, etc.

The conclusions and recommendations of the Commission will be based on in-depth studies of selected subjects carried out with the help of recognized experts and national or international bodies chosen from all parts of the world for their specialized knowledge or experience. In addition to direct input by experts in the form of policy-oriented research papers, the Commission also sponsors panel discussions or brainstorming sessions. Similarly, close contact is maintained with agencies dealing with subjects of interest to the Commission in order to avoid duplication of effort, complement ongoing projects and exercise a catalytic influence in promoting innovative solutions. Heads of these agencies or their representatives are invited to testify at the Commission's bi-annual plenary sessions.

The in-depth studies and expert advice received by the Commission have been instrumental in the preparation of sectoral reports on particular humanitarian issues which are published for public distribution in order to encourage timely follow-up action. The sectoral reports are addressed to policy-makers within governments, regional bodies, inter-governmental and private voluntary agencies and the general public.

The first sectoral report entitled *Famine: A Man-Made Disaster?* was published in 1985. The purpose of this report is to increase public awareness of the famine conditions afflicting much of Africa and the Third World, recommend positive solutions and facilitate further study and analysis of the situation. The report has already been published in eight languages.

Sectoral reports on deforestation and desertification (the present report) as well as on street children were published early in 1986. Additional reports on disappeared persons, humanitarian norms in armed conflict, refugees and other humanitarian topics are forthcoming.

The overall efforts of the Commission are thus a pyramid-like process which will culminate in the preparation of its Final Report scheduled for the end of 1986. The Final Report will address the humanitarian implications of a diverse range of global issues and set forth a viable framework for the implementation of a new international humanitarian order. It will be a policy and practice-oriented blueprint for effective response to the colossal challenge posed by humanitarian problems.

Members of the Commission

Sadruddin AGA KHAN (Iran) — UN High Commissioner for Refugees, 1965–77. Special Consultant to the UN Secretary General since 1978. Special Rapporteur of the UN Human Rights Commission, 1981: Founder-President of the Bellerive Group.

Susanna AGNELLI (Italy) — Under-Secretary of State for Foreign Affairs since 1983. Member of the Italian Senate. Member of the European Parliament, 1979–81. Journalist and author.

Talal Bin Abdul Aziz AL SAUD (Saudi Arabia) — President, the Arab Gulf Programme for UN Development Organizations (AGFUND). UNICEF's Special Envoy, 1980–84. Former Administrator of Royal Palaces, Minister of Communications, of Finance and National Economy, and Vice-President of the Supreme Planning Commission.

Paulo Evaristo ARNS (Brazil) — Cardinal Archbishop of Sao Paulo. Chancellor of the Pontifical Catholic University, Sao Paulo State. Author.

Mohammed BEDJAOUI (Algeria) — Judge of the International Court of Justice since 1982. Secretary-General, Council of Ministers, 1962–64; Minister of Justice, 1964–70. Ambassador to France, 1970–79; UNESCO, 1971–79; and the United Nations in New York, 1979–82.

Henrik BEER (Sweden) — Secretary-General of the League of Red Cross Societies, 1960–82. Secretary-General of the Swedish Red Cross, 1947–60. Member of the International Institute for Environment and Development and the International Institute of Humanitarian Law.

Luis ECHEVERRIA ALVAREZ (Mexico) — President of the Republic, 1970–76; Founder and Director-General of the Centre for Economic and Social Studies of the Third World since 1976. Former Ambassador to Australia, New Zealand and UNESCO.

Pierre GRABER (Switzerland) — President of the Swiss Confederation, 1975. Foreign Minister, 1975–78. President of the Diplomatic Conference on Humanitarian Law, 1974–77.

Ivan L. HEAD (Canada) — President of the International Development Research Centre (IDRC). Special Assistant to the Prime Minister of Canada, 1968–78. Queen's Counsel.

M. HIDAYATULLAH (India) — Vice-President of India, 1979–84. Chief Justice of the Supreme Court, 1968–70; Chief Justice of the Nagpur and Madhya Pradesh High Courts, 1954–58; Chancellor of the Jamia Millia Islamia since 1979. Former Chancellor of the Universities of Delhi, Punjab. Author.

Aziza HUSSEIN (Egypt) — Member of the Population Council. President of the International Planned Parenthood

129

Federation, 1977–85. Fellow at the International Peace Academy, Helsinki, 1971; the Aspen Institute of Humanistic Studies, 1978–79.

Manfred LACHS (Poland) — Judge at the International Court of Justice since 1967 and its President, 1973–76. Professor of Political Science and International Law. Former Chairman of the UN Legal Committee on the Peaceful Uses of Outer Space.

Robert S. McNAMARA (USA) — President of the World Bank, 1968–81; Secretary of Defense, 1961–68. President, Ford Motor Company, 1960–61. Trustee of the Brookings Institute, Ford Foundation, the Urban Institute and the California Institute of Technology. Author.

Lazar MOJSOV (Yugoslavia) — Member of the Presidency of the Socialist Federal Republic of Yugoslavia. Former Foreign Minister. Ambassador to the USSR, Mongolia, Austria, the United Nations, 1958–74. President of the UN General Assembly, 32nd Session and of the Special Session on Disarmament, 1978.

Mohammed MZALI (Tunisia) — Prime Minister and General Secretary of the Destorian Socialist Party. Member of the National Assembly since 1959. Former Minister of National Defence, Education, Youth and Sports and Health. Author.

Sadako OGATA (Japan) — Professor at the Institute of International Relations, Sophia University, Tokyo. Representative of Japan to the United Nations Human Rights Commission. Member of the Trilateral Commission.

David OWEN (United Kingdom) — Member of Parliament since 1966. Leader of the Social Democratic Party since 1983. Foreign Secretary, 1977–79.

Willibald P. PAHR (Austria) — Secretary-General of the World Tourism Organization. Federal Minister of Foreign

Affairs, 1976–83. Ambassador. Vice-President of the International Institute of Human Rights (Strasbourg).

Shridath S. RAMPHAL (Guyana) — Secretary-General of the Commonwealth since 1975. Former Attorney-General, Foreign Minister and Minister of Justice.

RU XIN (China) — Vice-President of the Chinese Academy of Social Sciences; Professor of Philosophy at the Xiamen University; Executive President of the Chinese National Society of the History of World Philosophies.

Salim A. SALIM (Tanzania) — Deputy Prime Minister and Minister of Defence. Former Prime Minister and Foreign Minister. Ambassador to Egypt, India, China and Permanent Representative to the United Nations. Former President of the UN General Assembly and the Security Council.

Léopold Sédar SENGHOR (Senegal) — Member of the French Academy. President of the Republic of Senegal, 1960–80. Cabinet Minister in the French Government before leading his country to independence in 1960. Poet and philosopher.

SOEDJATMOKO (Indonesia) — Rector of the United Nations University, Tokyo, since 1980. Ambassador to the United States. Member of the Club of Rome and Trustee of the Aspen Institute and the Ford Foundation.

Hassan bin TALAL (Jordan) — Crown Prince of the Hashemite Kingdom. Founder of the Royal Scientific Society and the Arab Thought Forum. Concerned with development planning and the formulation of national, economic and social policies. Author.

Desmond TUTU (South Africa) — Archbishop of Cape Town. Winner of Nobel Peace Prize. Former Secretary General of the South African Council of Churches. Professor of Theology.

131

Simone VEIL (France) — Member of the European Parliament and its President 1979–82; chairs the Legal Affairs Committee of the European Parliament. Former Minister of Health, Social Security and Family Affairs, 1974–79.

E. Gough WHITLAM (Australia) — Prime Minister, 1972–75; Minister of Foreign Affairs, 1972–73; Member of Parliament, 1952–78. Ambassador to UNESCO.

Titles on the Environment

Bina Agarwal
COLD HEARTHS AND BARREN SLOPES
The Woodfuel Crisis in the Third World
1986

Clyde Sanger
ORDERING THE OCEANS
The Making of the Law of the Sea
1986

A Report for the Independent Commission on International Humanitarian Issues
THE VANISHING FOREST
The Human Consequences of Deforestation
1986

A Report for the Independent Commission on International Humanitarian Issues
THE ENCROACHING DESERT
The Consequences of Human Failure
1986

Sue Branford and Oriel Glock
THE LAST FRONTIER
Fighting over Land in the Amazon
1985

Ted Trainer
ABANDON AFFLUENCE!
1985

Vaclav Smil
THE BAD EARTH
Environmental Degradation in China
1984

The above titles are available in both cased and limp editions, and can be ordered direct from Zed Books Ltd., 57 Caledonian Road, London N1 9BU. If you are interested in a full Catalogue of Zed titles on the Third World, please write to the same address.